Stoicism for Beginners

Practical Guide to Build Your Own Daily Stoic Routine and Achieve True Happiness

© **Copyright 2019 - All rights reserved.**

The content contained within this book may not be reproduced, duplicated or transmitted without direct written permission from the author or the publisher.

Under no circumstances will any blame or legal responsibility be held against the publisher, or author, for any damages, reparation, or monetary loss due to the information contained within this book. Either directly or indirectly.

Legal Notice:

This book is copyright protected. This book is only for personal use. You cannot amend, distribute, sell, use, quote or paraphrase any part, or the content within this book, without the consent of the author or publisher.

Disclaimer Notice:

Please note the information contained within this document is for educational and entertainment purposes only. All effort has been executed to present accurate, up to date, and reliable, complete information. No warranties of any kind are declared or implied. Readers acknowledge that the author is not engaging in the rendering of legal, financial, medical or professional advice. The content within this book has been derived from various sources. Please consult a licensed professional before attempting any techniques outlined in this book.

By reading this document, the reader agrees that under no circumstances is the author responsible for any losses, direct or indirect, which are incurred as a result of the use of information contained within this document, including, but not limited to, — errors, omissions, or inaccuracies.

Table of Contents

Chapter 1: Introduction 1

Chapter 2: A Brief History of Stoicism 3

    Ancient Stoicism 3

    Modern Stoicism 8

Chapter 3: Love, Death, and Money 12

Chapter 4: The Stoic Happiness Triangle 25

    In the Center: The Ideal, Eudaimonia, Well-Being, Core Beliefs 25

    Top of the Pyramid: Behavior 32

    Right Bottom of the Triangle: Emotions 33

    Left Side of the Bottom: Thoughts, Mind, Reason 35

Chapter 5: What Do I Really Control? 61

Chapter 6: The Stoic Way 68

    Open-Mindedness 68

    Humility 70

    Honesty 71

    Acceptance 72

    Willingness 74

    The World 75

Self-Restraint 78

Mindfulness.. 80

Chapter 7: The Stoic's Daily Regimen 83

Monday Morning – Open-Mindedness............................. 84

Tuesday Morning – Humility 85

Wednesday Morning – Honesty 86

Thursday Morning – Acceptance...................................... 87

Friday Morning – Willingness 88

Saturday Morning – The World.. 88

Sunday Morning – Self-Restraint 90

All Throughout the Day 93

In the Evening Before Bed 96

Chapter 8: Championship Stoicism 100

Practice, Practice, Practice... 100

The Ideal Stoic Practitioner 104

Always Practice Mindfulness 106

Forgiveness or Detachment 108

Self-Deprivation 114

Moderation.. 118

Memento Mori.. 120

Let Go of What Other People Think about You 122

Make Clear Goals but Don't Obsess over Results........... 124

Imagine Absence, Imagine What You Fear 127

Everything Is not as It Should Be: Count Your Blessings. 130

Chapter 9: Further Reading and Stoic Sayings 133

Some Further Reading 133

Some Quotes from Epictetus 134

Some Quotes from Marcus Aurelius 135

Some Quotes From Seneca 136

Chapter 1: Introduction

Who doesn't want to feel good? Who doesn't want always to have that sense of well-being that everyone experiences at various times in our lives? A sense of peace and tranquility, a sense that our life matters, a sense that what we do is significant?

The goal of Stoicism For Beginners is to get you acquainted with the fundamentals of the practice of Stoic philosophy and to give you a concrete program that will get you there not only once in a while but keep you there.

We'll first take a brief look at the history of Stoic philosophy.

Then we're going to cover some of the key concepts of Stoic philosophy. We'll see how they apply directly to anyone's life, no matter their specific circumstances so that you might keep that sense of meaning and tranquility flowing throughout all your days. As you'll see, Stoicism puts you on a clear pathway towards that sense of a life lived with purpose and significance, particularly when things are at their most challenging.

After discussing those key Stoic concepts, we'll see how they fit into an easy to understand and logical approach to life. We'll discuss why the world is the way it is, and most importantly, why each of us is the way we are in relation to that world.

What is it that I truly control? A crystal clear statement of this question and all its implications will then be the focus of our discussion. This key Stoic question will form the basis of our practice. This is just as it was for those first Stoics, over two thousand years ago, as it is for Stoics who live and practice today.

We'll provide you with a particular program of Stoic practice, which you can use every day to advance your life goals. You'll see how basic Stoic principles are timeless spiritual principles that are present in virtually all the world's great faiths. Put into practice in a coherent and thoughtful Stoic manner, they form an unshakeable edifice of daily practice that transforms lives.

Are you ready to get started?

Chapter 2: A Brief History of Stoicism

Ancient Stoicism

"An unexamined life is not worth living."

Stoicism develops from ancient Greek ideas that first gathered most prominently around Socrates and then Plato's Academy. Zeno, a merchant from Citium (modern-day Cyprus), is generally regarded as the founder of the Stoic school of philosophy in the early 3rd century BCE in Athens.

It's said that Zeno ended up in Athens because of a shipwreck. He was a prosperous merchant with a shipload of merchandise he intended to sell there, but apparently, the weather wasn't cooperative. Or maybe the captain had a little too much to drink. Regardless, the ship went down, and he lost everything. He barely escaped drowning. As the story goes, Zeno made his way, broke and probably a big mess, kind of like a homeless guy these days, to the agora of Athens, which was a sort of ongoing giant farmers market in Athens, the bustling center of life. It's said that Zeno observed later in life, "When I lost all my wealth coming to Athens, I, in fact, became a wealthy man."

Rather than a lamb skewer, though, it's said Zeno used his last few coins to buy a copy of the great sayings of Socrates. Perusing it, he then asked the bookseller, "Where is there a man like this?" The bookseller replied, "Well, Socrates is dead, long time ago. Poison or something. But ask him over there," He was pointing to a guy who looked like he was homeless, too. It was Crates, who was a practitioner of Cynicism, a philosophy which had broken off from The Academy, the school Plato had started.

Zeno started up a conversation with Crates, the Cynic. As the story goes, Zeno followed him for a while. But after a few years, Zeno became disillusioned with Cynic philosophy. It was, well, pretty cynical. Cynics thought everybody should go back to nature and live like dogs (kynes), quite literally, which is where the word Cynic comes from. It doesn't sound very appealing to me, either.

Zeno, in time, developed his own philosophy and would lecture on it from painted stoa (porches), from which Stoicism derives its name. Like Cynicism, it was rooted in the idea that philosophy should have practical applications for life as it's lived, mostly that one needs to live in accord with nature. But living like a dog in the street was taking it a little too far. But Zeno's new approach to an active philosophy was evidently well-received, and over time he garnered many followers, some wealthy, some not. He became popular among a few kings, too. He became successful, and his ideas traveled well beyond his lifetime, and were further developed among many ancient Greeks and then Romans.

It was through a man called Epictetus, a Greek slave in fact, and over a hundred years later, that we have the first direct written accounts of Stoicism. And even that was through one of Epictetus' pupils, Arrian. He apparently took excellent notes in class.

Like all schools of philosophy, Stoicism attempted to provide a coherent theory of the universe and of man's place within it. Based on these observations, Stoicism also presents a prescription for the manner in which an individual might live the best possible life. Ancient Stoicism put great store into an ethical plan for one's life, based upon a reasoned appreciation of the nature of the world as well as a frank assessment of an individual's place within it. It posits that man is intrinsically a social creature. But that also each individual is an island unto themselves.

A "general goo" and the peace of mind of an individual were inter-related. An individual should, indeed, strive to live a life of virtue in line with nature. The Stoic philosophy and its prescriptions for daily living caught on and became a widely popular school of philosophy as well as the manner of conduct.

Unlike much of Greek philosophy until around that time, Stoicism addressed the issues of daily life. How do I conduct myself with others? Upon what foundation of understanding should I act? And to what end? It's been suggested that to some degree, the emergence of Stoicism comes along with the emergence of modern consciousness. Who am I? What is my place in the universe? And, most importantly, if I'm going just to die someday, then why should I even care?

Stoicism addresses such questions by proposing a simple, clearly stated well. Human happiness (or well-being might be a closer translation of the Greek), derived from living in harmony with the flowing of life, a life whose very nature is change and constant flux. This is only possible with a sober application of reason, which, in turn, requires mastery over the unruly disturbances brought about by our emotional, instinct-based, reactions to the world around us. Emotions are often disruptive and turn us away from our reasoning capacities, our clear understanding of our true place in the universe, which is to play our role with virtue and in harmony with the world around us.

Such an understanding, they reasoned, should lead us to live moderately. Not to deny the needs or impulses of the body, but to give them their proper weight and to understand that indulgence beyond what is necessary cannot lead to happiness. It clouds the judgment and threatens to remove our actions from any possible wise and discernably good effect. The goal is not necessarily to deny feeling but to bring it into happy accord with our mind, the dominant faculty of reason, and so with all those others who live in the world around us.

Stoicism has perhaps been too closely associated with ideas of self-deprivation and self-flagellation, particularly in a Christian worldview, which came much later, with its notions of original sin. Such assumptions miss the point entirely. In fact, Stoicism was and is a philosophy that is concerned with the prescriptions for wresting the most satisfaction and deepest enjoyment from life. A sense of meaning and purpose in one's action, and of one's place in the world, any serious practicing Stoic could tell you, is the point of and product of a Stoic life.

Modern Stoicism

"Man can detach from immediate environments and choose

an attitude regarding himself, thus attaining inner freedom

and a basis for meaningful action."

- Victor Frankl

Stoicism and its precepts are enjoying a broad resurgence recently. Based upon renewed scholarly interest in Stoicism among 20th-century scholars, the basic Stoic ideas have been found to be quite applicable to the conundrums of 21st-century life. Some of the new Stoics are also actual scholars, people who study the received texts from various points of academic inquiry. Other modern Stoics are folks who've simply seen the logic and wisdom in the Stoic concepts, and how they benefit them in their lives. Indeed, there is a wide array of groups on social media that now share Stoic precepts and views on the Stoic lifestyle. There are numerous books about the practical application of Stoicism in daily life. There's even a "Stoicon" convention that now meets every year in differing locales all over the world with tens of thousands of attendees.

Earlier in the 20th century, and still today, Stoic concepts have been adapted to therapeutic theories broadly informing all manner of schools of therapy, thanks to such influential 20th century psychologists as Dr. Albert Ellis, Aaron T. Beck and, perhaps most notably, Viktor Frankl, who survived imprisonment in a Nazi concentration camp thanks to concepts and practices derived directly from the ancient Stoics. This is perhaps the most extreme example of the usefulness of Stoicism, and one which hopefully no one will have to experience again.

The core principle of Stoicism might be stated as follows: It's not what happens that troubles us, but our response to what happens. And over our response to events, we do in fact have control." Of course, this is easier said than done.

One key problem regarding Stoicism as a viable philosophy in the 20th century has to do with our understanding of nature, of the great changes in our perceptions of the nature of the world over the last two thousand years. We are a tiny species trapped upon a little rock in an ever-expanding universe, a universe that doesn't seem too much care whether we prosper or not. Science has also brought about technological changes that have resulted, among much good, in human inflicted suffering on mass industrial scales unimaginable in Zeno's time. Can such a philosophy work, based as it was upon archaic ideas of nature as a "good" in and of itself? Wasn't it then "nature" that developed nuclear weapons and Nazi concentration camps?

Aside from merely semantic arguments, it has been proposed that Stoicism's insistence than one life in accord with such a "Nature" can be usefully transposed into an insistence that one lives in accord with simply what is, with "the facts" of the world. Upon this foundation, Stoic precepts are still useful. Some would even suggest that Stoic precepts are even more pertinent now. They would suggest that acceptance of the world around one as it is, as our technologies allow for ever greater alienating consequences, is all that more important. Regardless, both then and now, as a practical application of a philosophy, the question is unchanged and might best be expressed like this: How do I live the best life within an everchanging flowing world as I can best understand it?

Needless to say, within the sweep of ancient Stoicism, which is 500 years give or take, and within modern Stoic practice today, there's considerable divergence. But it wouldn't be appropriate for our purposes to spend any more effort in detailing it. As you progress, though, you may very well want to investigate all these various threads and differing views.

For now, let's begin by observing that Stoics everywhere are deeply involved with the questions regarding individual agency. What exactly do I control? And what do I not?

Chapter 3: Love, Death, and Money

First off, let's bring Stoicism into the modern world. Let's posit three examples of life situations, some version of which everyone will find themselves in at one point or another. Let's think about those people who might be experiencing the following:

I didn't get that promotion I wanted, even though I worked my butt off for it and I was told if I did so I would get it. Three years of my life has gone down the drain. I should have taken that other job.

Then, after five years, I can't believe she would simply leave. After everything, I did for her. I totally changed my life, moved to a new city, and all of a sudden the person I'd thought I'd spend the rest of my life with said they're not interested. Oops, sorry for the inconvenience. I hate her. God, I really miss her.

And then my Dad, who I loved, just died. To top it off, he didn't even leave a will. Did he think he was going to live forever? And my brother started in about the money and the house even before he was put into the ground. What kind of respect is that? You know, I never really liked my brother. Of course, I love him to death.

And even if you're not one of those unfortunates above who seem to have just suffered a serious setback in life, you might very well be suffering, at least at times, from a more general, less defined malaise. It's safe to assume, at the very least, you haven't achieved perfect enlightenment, or you would never have picked any book of applied philosophy, let alone this one on the Stoic way. Of course, you might already be a Sage with quite developed ideas and practices. Most likely it's that you, like most of us, are some combination of all of the above. Certainly you will face the death of loved ones, and eventually your own death. You'll probably have had and will have money problems too, problems with work or business. And surely you'll have some, let's say, relationship issues as well. Let's face it; life can be pretty tough going sometimes.

Like everyone, you're neither entirely bad nor entirely good, but somewhere in the middle. What's important is which direction are you heading. The proposition of this book is to give you a clear pathway to the good. Given a clear choice most people, if given the opportunity to choose, say, at some abstract crossroads of life, a turn to bad or a turn to good, would surely choose the turn to the good. But what is the good? Can you define it?

The Stoics define the good as living in a harmonious state with the world, taking action guided by our faculties of reason. Which, again, is easier said than done. Marcus Aurelius, the Roman Emperor who lived in the 2nd century CE, and who is perhaps the greatest popularizer of Stoicism, said this: If you don't know what the world is, you can't know where you are. And if you don't know why the world exists, you can't know why you exist.

That's a pretty tall order these days. In essence, he's saying, what is the purpose of this world? What is my purpose in it?

It's really a question most of us would prefer to avoid. The modern world is full of endless distractions, and in fact, it's pretty easy to avoid the question, though it doesn't often lead to a very fulfilling or happy life. Even for a smart Greek living over 2,000 years ago, it was still a pretty tough one, but perhaps there were some easier answers to arrive at. Well, once the answer surely went, it's because Zeus is really mad at Hera again, that's why a thunderbolt destroyed my shack. Science indeed has little to say on questions of purpose. In place of Zeus being cranky again, it doesn't offer up any satisfying explanation for why my shack just got blasted away. Why my shack? It's going to cost a fortune to get a new one, at least four goats.

Yet, out of such a worldview can be derived a sense of purpose, which is to say my purpose is not to do anything that aggravates Zeus. Or, even better, to do things that might keep Zeus in a good mood. Like, say, giving him one of the goats in a sacrifice tonight (Of course I'll eat most of it anyway. I love barbequing goats with my buddies).

In explaining so many of the complexities of causal relationships that govern the world, science has left a thinking person somewhat bereft of core explanations. Why am I here? To what purpose? The why questions just aren't science's domain, pretty much only the how questions. Beats me, says science, not a very interesting question anyway. Read some philosophy.

Some modern Stoics suggest that the meaning, the why, and purpose of life, is in the search itself for meaning. Or it's in that sense of calm and well-being, perhaps, we have at times when contemplating a beautiful sunset; or the sense of well-being that comes with an act of generosity or kindness, or any right and unselfish action. For Aurelius nearly 2,000 years ago, it was expressed thus: "The purpose of a man is to live in useful harmony with the world, and he will thus obtain happiness, peace, and contentment."

What prevents us from doing so? Why do we always seem to be in conflict with someone or some situation? Why are we so often dissatisfied with what we have? Or so keenly aware that others have more? And in this world of almost unimaginable prosperity, why do I feel I don't have enough? Why is it that so often the world seems to offer up to us intolerable and bitter defeats? Why don't things happen as we wish them to happen? What am I doing wrong?

The ancient Stoics were human beings too, so we can safely assume they knew about frustration and unhappiness, that they feared death but also knew something about love. Human nature probably hasn't changed that much in 2,000 years, even though our knowledge of the world has.

Stoicism, then and now, proposes that all human unhappiness is the result of emotions run riot, unchecked, and most importantly of all, unseen and unexamined in the calm and clear light of reason. So much of our energy is wasted on trying to control things over which we have no control. Yes, Dad died. I didn't get the job. My marriage is over. We try to cover all these major disappointments with alcohol or drugs perhaps, or mindless consumption chasing elusive highs, or pointless distractions that rarely leave us with a real sense of well- being. Or we spend precious moments of our life in futile and furious remorse over events we had little control over in the first place. Or even if we did, they happened and can't be undone. But down into downward spirals of self-pity, we often fall when life's inevitable disruptions occur.

But even in our day to day life, just going to work or school, interacting with those we meet in life's casual encounters, do we not often fall victim to some similar disturbances in ourselves? That guy who just cut me off in traffic. The co-worker who might have been a little grateful when I offered to get her some coffee, instead of just barking out no. Or that girl who ignored me in the gym. Like, I wasn't even there.

How often are our time and energy wasted in petty resentment and anger? Perhaps it would have been easier to let the guy into the lane ahead of me. Maybe he's having a baby. Maybe my co-worker just got dumped by her boyfriend. Perhaps she's just about to jump out the window because she really liked him. Maybe the girl in the gym just didn't see me, was so zoned into her workout she didn't hear me say hi. So much of our actions, the little things we do or say, are based upon expectations that are ill-informed. But even if not ill-informed, even if based on a clear-eyed assessment of a situation, the time we waste responding in negative emotionally charged ways is self-defeating and really, if you think about it, absurd.

The fact is people just don't always cooperate. They don't seem to be reading from the script as I've prepared it in my mind. So what's wrong with them?

That is precisely the wrong question to ask. What's wrong with me, the Stoic is instructed to ask. How have I allowed all these people and circumstances to take away, once again, my peace of mind, my sense of well-being? How have I failed?

In the center of all this is ego run amok and self-centeredness so myopic as to be soul-killing, proposes the modern Stoic. It's tempting to think there's something unique about the modern world, and it may well be the case, that has heightened the illusion of disconnect between one's sense of entitlement and one's inability to wrest meaningful satisfaction from life. Imagine Zeno, or any ancient Greek for that matter, walking into a Walmart, facing the sheer volume of consumer goods and foods on display for easy and immediate purchase. It would be incomprehensible and mind-numbing for them. Several hundred types and flavors of just ice cream, for instance. How do you settle on just one?

Along with the laudable prosperity so many, but certainly, not all of us, enjoy, it can also seem at times to place us into heightened states of agitated uncertainty. We're overwhelmed and at times utterly baffled by the sheer volume of choice that confronts us in so many areas of life. If Walmart ran out of everything but, say, chocolate ice cream, there would be fears of an imminent riot. Or at least there'd be a lot of very unhappy customers who'd be shopping at the competition next week.

So while a good argument might be made that the way we've organized our modern world, with our dizzying array of consumer choice, actually promotes unhappiness, the Stoic proposal is firmly planted in an enduring problem of human nature. The confusion of an untrained intellect, baffled by endless choice in any age, is right at the core of our problem. It's not an exclusively modern problem but an enduring human conundrum. In a world of free will, how do I choose the right action among the seemingly infinite choices before me?

A program of useful living modeled upon Stoic concepts, in particular, suggests that it is in fact in my mind, in my intellectual experience of the world, that I have the greatest power of choice. Through the reasoned application of my mind, I'm not only able to direct my behavior, but also, ultimately, I'm able to influence my emotional responses and engagement as the world flows around me and as I flow with it. Once again, this is easier said than done. But anything worth truly rarely comes easily. Of course, I wouldn't mind winning the lottery this week. But it's unlikely, so I don't think I'll be making serious plans for that happening. Rather, I think I'm going for the sure thing, the thing that says I can be happy no matter what my specific circumstances in life are. Besides, don't most lottery winners end up broke and miserable?

And now we're starting to close in on something that's important for any practicing Stoic. What are my ideals? What is happiness or well-being to me? Does money equal happiness? Does love equal happiness? Would even immortality itself make me happy? The Greeks, from whom Stoicism was first articulated, had a vision of deity as forces as restless and discontented as human beings themselves. Sometimes just bored, sitting around binge-watching endless shows, eating and drinking too much, squabbling among themselves because, apparently, when you live forever nothing really matters all that much.

Is happiness a state of being derived from circumstances outside of my control? Or does it exist apart from the haphazard contingencies of life? What are the deeper springs from which happiness flows? Are they entirely within myself?

Here's a thought experiment. You're given a choice. Remember the best day of your life, when you felt the happiest you've ever been. Say, graduation. Or a wedding. Or just some moment when you were up in the mountains, in total peace and harmony with the world, enjoying some feeling of utter contentment. Do you have it in mind? Good.

Now let's say the choice you're given is between that sense of well-being lasting for the rest of your life, or you can have half a billion dollars to do with as you wish, but only under one condition. The condition is you'll be filled with anger, hatred, rage, and frustration for every hour of every day for the rest of your natural life. Getting the half-billion and being happy is not an option in this thought experiment. You will be miserable, like the worst day you ever had and for the rest of your life. But, then again, it's half a billion dollars.

So what's it going to be? The half-billion in misery or guaranteed peace and contentment? Are you a little conflicted? I am. I'd like to know what it is to have that kind of wealth. I could be really miserable on my Caribbean island, unhappy and bitterly frustrated as I lolled about in the sun by my pool. Another margarita and make it snappy this time you rotten little pool boy before I fire you. I think I'll blow my brains out. No, I can't, dammit, I got to live out this miserable life. Where's my f@#$ing margarita?!!

The Stoic sage, which this book is hoping you'll be on the path to being, wouldn't have to think long about the choice. He or she would choose contented usefulness without any regret whatsoever.

The key point we're trying to arrive at is this: happiness exists apart from any other contingency. This is a fundamental idea of the Stoic philosophy in practice. What is useful at this point is imagining and then being clear on this for yourself. It's going into the center of your triangle. What's the point of anything if it doesn't bring peace and contentment? It's an idea that the Greeks expressed as Eudaimonia, literally translated is something like well-spirited, or well-being. The Stoics of antiquity, over the course of several centuries, had a pretty developed program of how to achieve it. We modern Stoics probably have something close to the original idea. A life in harmony, free from strife, a life usefully lived, produces the greatest human happiness possible.

The impediment to this isn't the world around us, so uncaring and unfeeling regarding especially those things I want, but those roiling impulses within myself, the emotions, based on primal instincts, which come to color my mind's apprehension of the world and cause me to act in ways often regrettable, often harming others around me as well. And then it brings remorse which only compounds the frustration and unhappiness and further clouds the way I interpret the world, making my judgment faulty. We need to find a way to break this cycle. We need to think clearly.

To do so, it helps to picture the problem clearly. Let's take a look at The Stoic Happiness Triangle.

Chapter 4: The Stoic Happiness Triangle

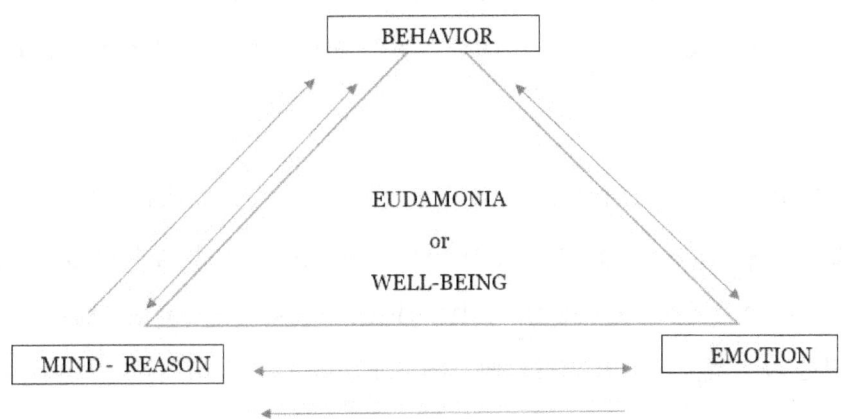

In the Center: The Ideal, Eudaimonia, Well-Being, Core Beliefs

"No man is free who isn't the first master of himself."

- Epictetus

We're determining that happiness is something apart from any external factors like wealth, fame, great job, great wife or husband, a really cool car, big lottery win, etc. Though of course, none of those things are bad in and of themselves, necessarily. The key concept is that we've understood that happiness is a state of being in and of itself, which exists apart from any of the outside conditions which may have brought it upon us.

It's to find the happiness that is our goal. We need to be absolutely, one hundred percent, crystal clear about this point.

It's not the things which we think may, or in fact have at times, have brought us to happiness. It's happiness itself that is the goal. Who doesn't want to be happy? Who wakes up in the morning saying I hope I have a terrible day today? What can I do to ensure I'm a miserable wreck today? And yet the key problem, which Stoicism recognizes and attempts to address as a practical philosophy, is that so much of what we do, in our day to day life, actually leads us straight into unhappiness and frustration. The human being seems so often an unhappiness machine. Our decisions both large and small, based upon self-interest alone and often animated by irrational fears, so often put us in collision with an uncooperative world, with others who probably aren't all that concerned with our happiness. Maybe others don't wish us harm. It's usually the case, although there will perhaps always be some who do.

But what others may intend, how they think, is simply not our concern.

The ideal of happiness, perhaps it's occurred to you, is enshrined in the very founding document of The United States. It's not the pursuit of wealth or dominion over others that are listed with the core values of life and liberty in our founding political document. It's the pursuit of happiness.

What can we say about happiness then? What does Stoicism say about it? Why can't I be in a state of happiness all the time?

It's a slippery notion, to be sure, happiness. The Greek term, eudaimonia, is perhaps a more useful way of expressing the concept. Happiness, in current usage, seems to have some connotations of euphoria, and hence of a temporary state of being which one inevitably comes down from. Like after eating that entire pint of chocolate ice cream from Walmart which you did end up buying since it was the only thing left on the shelf. The sugar crash was a real bummer, wasn't it?

"Happiness" is indeed what's promised along with virtually every consumer purchase we've ever made.

Food, of course. But also products like auto insurance. Change to Acme Auto Insurance, and you'll feel as wackily happy as me, promises the pitchman in every auto insurance commercial I've seen recently, as some wacky piano falls wackily from the sky.

So let's leave the term happiness out of it from here on out. Let's go with a closer translation of the Greek term eudaimonia, which is well-being. Well-being as in, I feel good, the universe and I are in sync. I'm right in the middle of it, in the zone, it's good, feeling the love and ready for whatever else comes my way.

The contrast between the two terms, happiness versus well-being, is more than mere nuance. It's critical. And perhaps particularly so for us, modern Stoics, who live in a world overwhelmed by a consumer-based economy with its constant appeals to our desires for self-gratification. Although our natural desire, as it's often expressed, is, of course, to be happy.

I can't get that song by Pharrell Williams out of my head either.

"...Because I'm happy

Clap along if you feel like happiness is the truth

Because I'm happy...."

-"Happy" by Pharrell Williams

Even though it's not as catchy, let's try to replace "because I'm happy" with "because I'm experiencing a sense of well-being" or even "because I'm living life in useful harmony with the world around me." For that matter, one wonders where we'd be if Jefferson had written among his self-evident truths and inalienable rights, that it was the pursuit of well-being rather than happiness which was so key to our identity.

Unlike happiness, the translation of eudaimonia as well-being also allows us to see more clearly the ethical dimensions upon which depend our ideal state of being.

The Stoics saw clearly that man was a social animal, that his highest purpose and deepest identity derived from his status as a social creature, a member of a group such as a nation, a tribe or a family, or as an individual in relation to other individuals, a mother or father, son or daughter, a colleague or a friend. Yet the Stoics also saw clearly that each person was an individual as well, and most importantly, an individual whose only true realm of direct control and influence was over himself or herself. An individual's primary obligations and responsibilities begin and end with himself or herself.

Such a concept doesn't imply that one lives without regard for others. Rather, it's quite the opposite. A Stoic manner of living is pointedly to fit oneself to be of maximum usefulness to the world, to those others around him or her, and that therein lies the true sense of well-being we all seek. We are, in our deepest souls, social animals. Our sense of well-being is tied to our relationships with others.

Perhaps this seems contradictory at first. So what you're saying is that the Stoic's primary responsibility is to himself, but it's so he can be of use to everyone else? That just doesn't make sense.

But it does when one considers another of the key tenets of Stoicism. The Stoic believes that a true apprehension of the world leads to one inescapable conclusion, that he controls very little of the world around him. Even the Stoic Marcus Aurelius, an Emperor of Rome no less, with Roman Legions awaiting his command to go pacify or conquer, saw clearly the limits of his ability to directly control the outcomes of events around him. This wasn't and isn't an admission of the futility of individual action, but rather an acceptance of reality. And it's with a clear-eyed view of reality that any potential meaningful action is based. The Stoic isn't freed from the obligation to act in an ethical manner. The Stoic is, however, obligated to try to exercise the best of his or her judgment in contemplation of action. This is something clearly within his or her control.

And so we live in an ever-changing world whose events even a Roman Emperor concedes we can do little to control. And yet our sense of well-being requires us to live in some kind of harmony with it, that we rightly relate ourselves to this world. Easier said than done. But whoever said life was easy?

We arrive at the center of the triangle: Eudaimonia. Let's just call it "well-being" at this point, while conceding that there's no perfect, single-word expression of the concept. In fact, you may very well wish to meditate often upon the subject yourself as a Stoic practitioner. But it's our bulls-eye, our goal.

Top of the Pyramid: Behavior

So why then do so many of the things I do seem to end up with me not experiencing a sense of well-being? After all, it's my behavior, which I control more than anything else in the world. How I act towards, and what I say to, all those I encounter in my life is the very thing I'm in complete control of. But when I look back honestly at my life, at any portion of it, my childhood, the last few years, yesterday, I can only see many instances of unhappiness and frustration. One goal of a practical application of Stoic philosophy should be to understand, through developing habits of honest examination, how exactly I've contributed to each and every instance of unhappiness and frustration.

There's an old adage that goes something like this: Every time I'm disturbed the problem is within me.

It's through our behavior with others around us that we express ourselves and take our place in the world. That's obvious, of course. But why should we allow the behavior of those others around us to disturb us? And at what point is our behavior, what we might say off the cuff in a stressful situation at work, for instance, contributing to further confusion and strife, causing others to react even more recklessly, leading us away from well-being.

A key goal in practicing a Stoic philosophy is to bring our behavior and actions, the things we say, into a useful concordance with the world around us. Let us at least not contribute to the strife. Let us rather conduct ourselves in a manner that aims to produce harmony among those around us, to the best of or ability.

Right Bottom of the Triangle: Emotions

The very definition of the word stoic in common usage today is an adjective that describes one who is in control of their emotions, calm and steady in the face of unfortunate or stressful situations. We all have emotions, of course. We wouldn't be human otherwise. Emotions influence us constantly, lead us to take certain postures, think certain ways, motivate our actions and behavior, and not always in negative ways. Behavior that flows from the natural feelings of love that a parent has for a child, of course, can hardly be said to be destructive. Or just the warm feelings of camaraderie we experience with friends we enjoy and care for, and in turn, inspire in them.

But of course, our behavior can be influenced by our emotions in other ways not quite as attractive. When threatened, like any cornered animal, we often lash out with our claws or bark out commands and threats, or worse. Who among us hasn't said or done things we immediately regretted afterward, wishing the moment to be replayed so that we might do or say something different? We often say or do hurtful things, especially to those closest to us, those we purport to love and cherish above all. And may the gods help that guy who just cut me off. Or whoever it was that forgot to restock the ice cream freezer last night.

Our emotions seem the wild card in our lives. Lenses that fall over us and through which we see and respond to the world, and yet we seem to have so little control ever so often.

The Stoic philosophers saw this problem as one of pleasure versus aversion. That within our emotional world, it was possible to divide everything that comes from our more animal natures as either drawing us towards pleasure or leading us to avoidance. Fear or love, to be the most reductive, perhaps. Attraction or repulsion, too. Neither one, as a basis for our actions, our behavior, was a sound foundation.

Left Side of the Bottom: Thoughts, Mind, Reason

And then there's that most uniquely developed part of the human being, the human mind, with all its capacities for thought and reason. Dependent, or even imprisoned you could say, within a human body and all the animal instincts to which a body is prone, it is nevertheless the singular tool whose development is without par in the natural world. It's our key to freedom.

But don't get too caught up in how great this mind of yours is. The Greeks had a word to describe the person who thought to have a mind made them into some kind of god. The word is hubris, and it means something like a lack of humility. And the real gods like Zeus really didn't like it when mortals started thinking they were like them. It got their blood boiling, and next thing you know, your shack and your goats are going to get hit by one nasty thunderbolt.

However, in the three points of the triangle we finally arrive at a point of entry where we can most decisively influence those things within ourselves we do have the most control over, and through which we're able to transform our lives into something like what we've placed in our triangle's center, eudaimonia, well-being, purpose.

After all, wasn't it through the use of our mind and its reasoning capacities that we've built the triangle in the first place? We've determined that above all we wish to live a useful and contented life, that our central goal of well-being derives from doing so, our deepest and truest self is there tucked away in that triangle's center.

This wasn't an understanding that our emotional selves brought us to. If I were a purely emotional animal, I'd just shoot you and take your stuff, your mate who I kind of like anyway, if I could get away with it. He is kind of hot. Our mind recognizes we are emotionally driven animals. Our mind also recognizes that if I were to do something so horrendous, I couldn't really live with myself, that such a life would be pointless and not worth living. Our mind recognizes the conundrum of human life. We're entirely social creatures living in individual and self-contained units.

Panta Rei is the famous observation of Heraclitus. Everything is flowing; everything is in motion. That seems most particularly to include us. We're born, and then we die. Others follow. Not just human beings but the very nature of the universe itself is one of constant change and ceaseless transformation. It was one of the great observations of the Greeks regarding the nature of reality, subsequently confirmed by science in countless ways. We're still roiling from this knowledge. Then who or what am I, here for only an instant?

Rather than digesting this difficult truth, then throwing in the towel, the Stoics took it in and saw not only was life still worth living, but saw how such knowledge applies to myself and to how I understand myself and how I might fashion a sweetly and deeply meaningful life around such a bummer of an idea. Even if you believe in such ideas of life after death, say a Christian cosmology, it doesn't matter. Stoicism gives you a plan for living a better life while you're here, that's the important point. Stoics are Christian, Jewish, Muslim, Hindu, and Buddhist. In fact, the practice of Stoic principles is entirely congruent with all manner of existing faiths.

It starts with the mind. The very part of our self we've exercised to arrive at our ideal, the center of the triangle.

In our triangle, we see a flow between three divisions of human experience. Thoughts flow into behavior as well as emotion. Emotions flow into behavior, which in turn flows into thoughts. Over behavior, we have absolute control, theoretically. But is that really always the case? As we've suggested above, don't we often do and say things we regret. Few among us are saints.

Just as Heraclitus noted the ever-changing nature of the universe around us, you could say that Stoicism recognizes that within us as well exists a flowing between differing parts. Our goal is to find a smooth flowing, free of disturbance, and to align that flowing within our self, as best as possible, with that greater flowing all around us.

Again, the entry point is the mind. We've made a gigantic leap forward in determining to our satisfaction what our goal is, well-being. Let me now assume that in a good and orderly way (you could say Christian, Hindu or pick your faith kind of way) you would like to extend this vision of yourself to all those around you. You wish them to know well-being as well. Even the guy that didn't restock the ice cream. He knows not what he did anyway.

But to what point do we really control our mind, the way we think, what we think about, even the conclusions we arrive at about the world? Most of us, including yours truly, upon a frank and honest examination, would have to say not as much as I'd like to. I vote a certain way because my parents did. I believe certain things to be true because it's in my interest to believe them. Yet most of us profess to have opinions, some quite deeply held. We have convictions too, rock-solid core beliefs that we'd fight to defend. Yet in the end, there's, in fact, a considerable amount of ego invested in what we claim as our beliefs. A key Stoic virtue is an open-mindedness, a willingness to change one's views when presented with or arriving at a better understanding. If you think about it, over-attachment any one particular view of the world can seem, at a time, a little close-minded.

The modern Stoic's first enemy we'll call ego, for lack of a better term. You could also use words such as self-centeredness, undue pride. If I do an honest examination of those past events which have disturbed me, brought me into self-pity and unhappiness, I'll often find that I participated to some degree or other in making them worse. I acted under the guise of outraged self, egocentrically, with undue pride. Now here's the key point. Even if I was blameless, the mere fact that I spent days or even years of my life in resentment and anger over the alleged perpetrator of the offense, is my fault. I'm, in fact, the one to blame. I've failed to accept reality and then squandered precious hours and energy of my life going over, and over, and over again, something I can never change. It happened. Case closed.

The Stoics had much to say on the topic of Virtue. And in many ways, we have been and are now discussing this concept. Let's look at the center of our pyramid again. Let's replace well-being with the word virtue; give it a clear ethical connotation. I'm in a state of well-being when I'm virtuous. Now here's the really big leap of Stoicism. If I live in a state of anger and resentment, even if I'm not to blame for the car crash, one hundred percent not my fault, I'm still to blame because it's impossible to act virtuously when I'm seething with resentment and anger. Emotions are like that. They bypass the mind and go right into a behavior. I'm going to take it out on someone and then bye-bye well-being. I'm a useless miserable wreck of a human being.

And the car crashes of life will happen. It's called the law of averages. Some unpleasant things, however, are absolutely guaranteed. People I love will die. People will fail to follow my script of life, deny me the things I've unfortunately placed my sense of well-being upon having. I won't get the job I want. I don't have as much money as I'd like. My girlfriend fell in love with a total douche. There will only be chocolate ice cream. And to top it all off, I'm going to die, and life has no meaning.

But this is what's really happening; the Stoic sage might point out. You're living in fantasy land. You've exchanged what did, in fact, happen, for what you would have liked to have happened. Your expectations about the world, and about your role in the world, what the world owes you, have come almost entirely from emotional impulses. Maybe you changed what you've put into the center of your triangle, without first consulting the mind. Or perhaps the mind was consulted, but only in the most perfunctory way. Your emotions bullied your mind out of the way, forced it to concede to the childish demands of ego-driven self-centeredness. Most likely, you just went straight to behavior, acted out foolishly. It's my way or the highway, with a sharp elbow thrown. Even though there's plentiful evidence that such behavior rarely, if ever, ends well for you.

Fear is a basic instinct, quite useful. It keeps us from running out into busy intersections. Fear tells us when we've reached the limits of safety while driving. It tells us to be particularly careful while packing up our parachute before that first skydiving trip, to double and then triple-check that ripcord. It tells us even, at times, that it's probably best to not say that thing on the tip of your tongue to your wife just now, best to think it over a bit or wait for a different occasion.

In the scale of human evolution, however, it's not been all that long since we were chasing mastodons on the prairie. It's not been that long since the threat of a sudden lion attack was an issue we dealt with on a regular basis.

Yet fear still drives every aspect of our lives. In some ways quite obvious, other ways not so much. And this is where things get a little tricky. Fear not only works looking out for the obvious threats to immediate personal safety, but it's also often in cahoots with our mind, the one thing we thought we could trust. Fear is quite aware of the mind as it goes along, making its observations about life. It can even project into the mind's most serious business, which is contemplating the future, what we might expect to happen, what's coming down the pike and what we need to get ready for. Did you think about what might happen if - that is fear -

and there are a lot of ifs. Unless you're ready to be that Stoic sage living alone up in that cave in the mountains, with water and canned goods to last a lifetime (I wouldn't recommend it), I'm going to assume that as a modern Stoic you're still going to make decisions based upon future projections, you're going to try to achieve the goals of the center of the triangle.

The solution to the problem begins to appear now. It's funny how that works. The problem, once clearly apprehended, begins to suggest a solution. And in many ways, the Stoic path is about developing the capacities to see the problem as it truly is, whatever it is, in its true nature. Fear, in all its various forms of anger, envy, undue pride, resentment, and greed, among others, isn't stupid. After all, it's got a pretty good mind it's privy to. But, in the final analysis, it will be relegated to its proper role by a mind guided by a firm and resolute goal. Those goals and ideals, for instance, expressed in our triangle's center.

Let's return to our three examples from Chapter 3.

Lisa, our potential Stoic practitioner, didn't get a job she worked long and hard for, several years, in fact, to put herself into a position to claim. She did everything possible to demonstrate her capabilities as a team member in her stupid job, even excelled, and she'd been told, as a team leader. Her evaluations were first-rate. Her boss gave her every indication that it was going to happen for her, seemed to take special pride in her performance, said she was her number one, called upon her often for special tasks she assured her only she could be trusted with.

Now, going to work every day in her crappy cubicle while Jason, the moron who ended up with the job sits in his office, gabbing away on the phone, taking day-long lunches with the corporate team, drives her crazy. Worst of all, Jason is kind of her boss now. At least, he thinks so. Something about his attitude is intolerable. She's looking for another job. But does she really want to move to a new gig, start all over again. Sharon, her real boss, the traitor, did say her time was coming. There's that. But how can Sharon be trusted?

Wow, Lisa really got screwed over. To work diligently three years, with a clear understanding of a solid promotion, and then for it not to happen. That's just wrong.

It's not the purpose of this guide to hand out career advice. But rather our purpose is to suggest how practicing Stoic principles can help anyone, even a very angry and frustrated Lisa, get back on board with a calm, contented, and useful life. First off, it seems clear that Lisa took a job that she probably didn't much want to be doing anyway. Which, let's face it, is a lot of many of us. Or if she did want to do it, she saw it as a means to an end. The job would have meaning for her only if it led to where she hoped it would lead, to that office with a nice view and a big bump in salary. Do you know what rents are these days? Lisa was, in fact, wasting years of her life living a provisional life. In the center of her triangle was "promotion," with all the prestige and happiness she assumed would come along with it.

A Stoic approach to work, even the kind of work Lisa is fortunate enough not to have to consider, like maybe working at a Starbucks, is that all work has dignity and offers immediate and daily rewards beyond a paycheck. The simple satisfaction of being a member of a team, for instance, or of providing a useful item like a nicely made latte, or of simply having an opportunity to make someone else's day a little better with a smile or a warm hello. When we spend our energy focusing on how we might serve others rather than what's to our advantage, we've left the world of ego-driven emotion and begun behavior that will only stabilize our triangle, get us to our goal. Here, behavior informed by the mind, what we've formulated in the center of our triangle, in fact, has a stabilizing effect upon the triangle's flow. With time and repeated practice, we even begin to influence our emotional responses. People tend to smile back when smiled at. And even when they don't, that's okay too.

Also, from what I heard around the water-cooler, Lisa could be a little stand-offish with Jason over the past year, definitely saw him as threat number one to her dream of the promotion. She did a few things that seemed a little underhanded. In fact, even Lisa is a little disappointed in herself for not notifying Jason that a deadline on a big project had brought forward.

Will Lisa get the next big promotion? Who knows? Certainly, Lisa doesn't know. The question really is this: Is she going to continue being unsettled and unhappy, seething in resentment over Jason and Sharon? This is clearly within her power to do something about. But if she gets that new job, won't the same pattern just repeat itself all over again in her new work environment? There will be more anxiety over promotion or status. Even if she got the promotion, the nice office, odds are Lisa would be right off focusing on the next move, up to corporate, the corner office upstairs.

But now here's the key and basic idea. Lisa isn't living in the present tense of life. She's in the future, on that promotion, and she's in the past, what didn't happen. To be honest, she's not that much fun to be around, and even she knows it herself. She needs to figure out what's in the center of her triangle, be absolutely clear about it, and then take the concrete steps not to get there, but to stay in it, because she's already there the moment she decides what it is. It might even help her in her career to get it out of the center of the triangle.

Resentments are deadly killers just like certain germs are. They're infections brought on and nourished by fear, fired into conflagrations by our inflated ego and our foolish insistence that the world conform to our desires. A big piece of Stoic philosophy concerns our proper attitudes towards others. Marcus Aurelius observes, "How much trouble we avoid when we don't look around to see what our neighbor does or thinks, but only concern myself with I think myself, that I might act rightly." This observation clearly doesn't pertain to not being aware of the well-being of others, but rather that our true and proper concern, in matters of personal ethical conduct, is me and myself only. Upon such a foundation can a firm foundation for living be built.

Joseph has been having a pretty tough week. His girlfriend, his fiancée, whatever she was, Lauren, man! He can barely even say her name—moved out last week. She just went up and left. Took her stuff, the cat, and a whole bunch of books, half of which he paid for himself. She left a note telling him not to call her for a month or so, she needed time, it was best this way, and that she was sorry, she at least said that. For sure, things hadn't been going that great the past year or so. But he did follow her all the way out here when that new job came up for her.

He's been inside, holed up, pretty much the whole week now, except for a few trips to the store to buy food and beer. Well, it's a pretty big deal to move halfway across the country for someone. He can't believe she'd do him like that. He needs another beer. Maybe something harder today. Though he really needs to get some work done. Thank goodness he works from home. Thank goodness nobody has to see him like this. God, he misses her, he thinks as he breaks down and cries again, umpteenth time today. Buck up, man.

He knew that Max guy wasn't just a "friend from work." Something was going on there right off.

If you've ever been through a breakup, you don't need Max, me, or anyone to tell you how bad it can get. Roiling feelings of self-pity, anger, bitter resentment are just the beginning. Life doesn't get much worse. Nothing lets our emotional life take control like the feelings which accompany a breakup, particularly a bad one, with hurt feelings around things which probably should haven't been said in the first place. We become that infant left in the woods, whose most basic instinct is to scream out with every ounce of energy, I'm here, I'm over here. Have you abandoned me? Don't you know there's a bunch of wolves around? Don't you know I'm utterly defenseless without you? I really don't want to die. Why did you leave me here?

Joseph is in for an extended period of mourning. Maybe he'll end up moving back to wherever he came from. Or maybe he won't. One thing is for sure. Life is going to move on with or without him. He can continue to drink himself into oblivion all alone in his apartment, or he can get back on the horse and get over it. The world doesn't really care which one it is. He might be bawling all alone in the woods, but the simple fact is that he's not an infant but a grown man.

Had Joseph been a practicing Stoic, however, he'd probably have developed some habits of mind and a daily life routine which would serve him very well during this difficult time, accelerate his return to daily contentment. Or, even more pointedly, Joseph most likely would never have reached the low point he's now in the first place.

Modern Stoic practice focusses sharply on developing a sense of what we'll call mindfulness. Through daily routines of meditation and reflection, as well as a practice of restraint and pause before acting or speaking when disturbed, let's call it "stepping back," certain habits of behavior begin to form which have a calming effect on the triangle's flow. For instance, when Lauren came back from work the first few months of her new job, she'd often be a little stressed from all the demands of a new job. It would seem like Joseph was the first friendly face she'd seen all day, someone to whom she could talk about all the events of the day, get clear in her own mind through talking to Joseph— her boyfriend—for god's sake, what had happened, what she was feeling, what it all meant.

The problem for Joseph was so often it seemed, to him, like just so much barking. He'd brush her off, say he had a project due soon. Or he'd make little jokes maybe. And come off condescending. Well, that's why I work from home. My boss is Fred; he's a cat, he'd say pointing to the cat who's now gone out of his life forever, too. Maybe it was funny to him, but for Lauren, the last thing she wanted was laughs. She just wanted to be heard.

For obvious reasons, ancient Stoicism doesn't have a lot to say specifically about modern relationships. How we marry and date and mate has changed considerably since then, and for the good one might observe. Yet virtually every practicing modern Stoic happily reports very positive changes in all their personal relations, and most specifically their romantic ones, once they began their daily practice of Stoic principles.

Amid the uncertain and anxious blabbing of his partner Lauren, had Joseph chosen a certain detachment and just listened to her, paid attention to what she was saying, instead of playing it off like a joke, or something annoying, the result for not only himself but also his partner would have been more positive, might have deepened and strengthened their relationship.

Of course, maybe it was destiny that Lauren was going to get together with Jason no matter what Joseph did. Sometimes relationships just end. Life often doesn't conform to our expectations. And maybe, in his heart of hearts, Joseph was ready for a new start as well, maybe he was pushing things in that direction without even knowing it. Either way had Joseph been striving to maintain mindfulness, his triangle would maybe not be entirely turbulent free, but he would have invaluable self-knowledge that would be guiding his actions, his behavior. Maybe he could have handled the end stages of a relationship more gracefully, with minimal damage. Now he's just stuck in a mess of grief, anger, and jealousy. Odds are, after unnecessarily wallowing in self-pity for a long time, he'll finally get over it but go on to make similar mistakes in his next chance at love.

Daily expressions of gratitude are one key way in which a modern Stoic can achieve well-being. What do I have to be thankful for? This can be as simple as going over a list in one's mind before sleep. Joseph, after all, did love, Lauren. They had some great times together. Did he bring this to the forefront of his mind on a daily basis? Probably not. Now that it's over, is Joseph going to simply file away the entire relationship as waste, something to be avoided thinking about at all costs? Probably. Except for those times to come when he's mired again in self-pity, he needs something to justify his general train of thought that the world has been so cruel to him. And I loved her too, might be that refrain. Joseph just isn't living in reality. If he were, perhaps he'd be able to accept this chapter in his life for exactly what it was, no more, no less. Perhaps he'd even be able to include his time with Lauren in his list of things he was grateful for having. The past is over. Is there something we might learn from it if we take the time to make an honest examination?

The practicing modern Stoic lives in the present tense of the current moment. Through habits of daily reflection and meditations, guided by the mind, he or she learn as they progress through life. Everything that has happened can inform the decisions made today. We make use of the past, and don't let it use us. As soon as it becomes the past, the past becomes a source of instruction to apprehend better and live the present moment, where life happens. The past isn't a source of grief or remorse, but an irrevocably closed chapter that offers invaluable knowledge.

Don's dad just died, suddenly, a heart attack. Don's mother died when he was young, and his dad never remarried. But Don's dad was a great dad, really stepped up and made him and his brother, John, his top priority in life. He helped him and John navigate the death of their mother under what must have been pretty tough times for himself, being a single dad and all. He was actually an amazing dad. He misses him. How would he handle this mess?

Don found out as he was checking his phone after getting off a plane. The text from John was direct, brutally direct: "Dad just dropped dead. Heart attack. Thought you'd like to know." Needless to say, after that stunning moment, then talking to John, taking it all in, he got the first flight back home, even though it was a big closing he just screwed up by bailing out at the last second.

That was a month ago. He and John had been squabbling a little before dad died—their relationship was always like that, so competitive, fighting for dad's limited attention probably—and things have definitely not improved between them since.

Dad didn't leave a will, any clear instructions regarding his estate, not huge but not insignificant either. The house, free and clear now, 401K, some other accounts. Lots and lots of paperwork before any distribution. But luckily it was just him and John, the clear beneficiaries. Or so he thought, until yesterday, when some other claimants suddenly popped up—a live-in girlfriend, really, or more like live-on—like jackals fighting over a carcass. If it goes to probate, gets contested, well then there goes most of it. And that seems to be the end result if John gets his way. This is tough. He and John are meeting at the attorney's office in a few minutes. Don's pulling up right now. And Don's going to put his foot down, right here, right now. No more bullshit.

Don walks into the office. John's already there, sitting down. The attorney, who John found, who's getting four hundred an hour, she's getting her cut for sure, is at her desk. Don says hi to John, who nods back as he sits down.

Our friend Don sounds a little stressed out. That's not good. He's in a pretty important and consequential meeting, and he doesn't seem to have a clear idea of what he wants out of it. The meeting could go a few different ways, of course, some more in his favor and some less so. What Don isn't clear on is what he considers his favor. Or even what his motivations are, what he'd like to achieve. Is it simply maximum money for himself? Is that what's going to lead him to the center of the triangle. Maybe. Maybe not. Don's pretty clueless here. He's never really thought anything through. The center of his triangle is, well, he doesn't know. Obviously, things aren't great with his brother, John. It doesn't sound like they have an entirely trusting relationship, a clear understanding between them. And also the sudden death of his dad, who sounded like a great guy, probably the one guy he could trust most in the world, isn't around any longer to help guide him. I have a sense this meeting isn't going to go well. Don's not leaving with a sense of well-being, to say the least.

How often do we try to control the uncontrollable? And how often we end up frustrated and baffled, even when engaged in life's daily routines. How can we then possibly be surprised by the swampy bewilderment we find ourselves mucking around in when life's most consequential moments appear before us? When are the stakes highest?

Don, still surely reeling by his father's sudden demise, not trusting his brother, particularly in this present situation, is his own worst enemy. If only, before he found himself in this meeting, in this present moment, he had some compass to guide him, some understanding of what his core motivations were, what he truly wanted, he'd be able to walk away from it in an hour's with a sense of calm regardless of the outcome. It's what his father would have wanted. In fact, his father expended considerable energy trying to get his two sons to appreciate each other, what they meant to each other, and to stop bickering all the time.

First off, a daily practice of Stoic principles would have brought Don to a clear understanding regarding his brother. It wouldn't have necessarily resulted in total comity between them. That would have been out of Don's control, though it may well have done so. Don was all too often to respond negatively in kind to what he was always very quick to perceive as John's petty and stupid needling. At the very least, though, there would have been clear communication between them. Don would have understood where John stood, and John would have understood where Don stood. Right now, before the meeting with the attorney, they would have had a frank and honest conversation, an understanding between them. Maybe Susan, the live-in girlfriend, Dad, after all, did once say how grateful he was for her, should be offered something. Dad would have probably wanted that.

But that didn't happen. Like always, Don avoided uncomfortable discussions with others as well as himself. Until it all just explodes out, similar to what is about to happen in an attorney's office who charges four hundred an hour. Who wouldn't watch people fight if they're making four hundred an hour doing it? But just as he and his one and only brother, the one person in the entire world who can see the other in the entirety of their life, need each other the most, they seem to be splitting further apart. And after all, what is said is done, after money is distributed and spent on home upgrades or whatever, the facts will remain the same. They each have one brother in this world. The stakes of this meeting are high; the money is just a symbol, really. There's something much larger at stake. Will this relationship further deteriorate? Or will it strengthen? Who is Don, and what does he value in his deepest parts. What can Don do to move it towards strengthening?

And here's the key point. Even if Don has a moment of clear understanding, miraculously becomes a sudden Stoic sage, and does, in fact, begin at this moment to act and speak thoughtfully, with both his brother's well-being and his father's wishes foremost in mind, the meeting could still be a disaster. Even if Don were that Stoic sage, master of his emotion and swami of perpetual well-being, the meeting could set off chains of events that left him with nothing, John angrily blaming him and wishing to never speak to him again. The live-in girlfriend got everything, maybe. But Don had conducted himself with wisdom, humility, and acceptance throughout the entire affair. He left the meeting that day in perfect repose. Like always, he felt deep gratitude for having had such a wonderful father. And for John as well, his brother who he loves. Hopefully, he'll come around. Don misses having him around.

How do we live a life in gratitude for what we have, rather than in a state of confusion and agitated uncertainty, with regret over what we don't have, what we've failed to get?

Wait a minute. How is it even possible to regret not having something?

It's really a nonsensical notion. If we examine this sentence closely, we, in fact, can gain some insight into one way our roiling emotional responses to the world lead us into all manner of conflict with the world as it is all around us. It's a common denominator of all three of the protagonists in our stories.

Chapter 5: What Do I Really Control?

Let's take a close look at that sentence; we regret what we don't have. It doesn't seem entirely unusual at first, conjures up what seems a coherent and relatable idea at first glance. Or at least it conjures up a state of mind that we can relate to. I regret, for instance, that I didn't take more STEM classes when I was in college. Every new development in physics or cell biology baffles me a little. I don't have a strong background in the basics of those sciences to understand all the implications of the discovery. At what point does regret over a past failure transfer to the present? I regret that in my present moment I don't have a strong STEM background

I also regret, for that matter, that I don't have the money to buy a Tesla, that S model I hear is pretty amazing, goes zero to sixty in a few seconds, and you don't hear anything. I also regret that I didn't ask a certain person to marry me twenty years ago. Man, I feel like crap. I'm still driving a Corolla, and my marriage was a disaster. If I get a Tesla—I could probably just barely make the payments, that is if I gave up food for two weeks every month, it's doable—

maybe I'd look better to that intriguing new lady who just moved next door.

Yet regret also sneaks its way into the future. I regret that I won't ever have better STEM knowledge or that Tesla. We're getting into the crazy country here.

Regrets evidently come in a few different varieties. There's regret for actions omitted as well as actions taken. There's also, evidently, a more general regret that can include all those things I don't have that I would like to have. And that's where we can begin to see most clearly the absurd nature of regret in the first place. Don't think advertisers and marketers aren't deeply aware of this either. How many pitches are made that aim directly at this sense of general regret? A lot, if you look closely. You don't have a Tesla, do you? Well that's a problem, right? It's only the coolest car in the world. Do you know what it feels like to get to sixty miles per hour in three seconds? What's wrong with you?

What is regret anyway? Put simply it's lament or remorse over something that happened or didn't happen, in the past. That's bad enough, wasting time and energy ruminating over unchangeable past events.

Yet somehow tricky little childish emotions, those fear-driven but intrepid toddlers of our triangle, just seem to take over and project themselves into our present moments of actual life. And boy they just make a big mess of things as toddlers do. They even, somehow, seem to be able to project themselves into the future. And that's really crazy. I so deeply regret that I will not own a Tesla in the future. It just breaks my heart. Yep, that's crazy.

Regret doesn't seem to be a very useful state of mind. Even when it's performing its prescribed dictionary function, lamenting something in the past, it just doesn't seem to get me anywhere I truly want to go. I really want to stay in the middle of my triangle. I've already determined that's it not only where I'm the most content, but it's also where I'm most useful to everyone around me. People like me most when I'm there. The center of the triangle is where life happens.

So how do we get rid of regret, and its playmates' lament and remorse? Well, we've just taken a gigantic step in doing so. We've identified it, unmasked them as the devilish little toddlers they are. Goodbye, regret, lament, and remorse. Have a nice nap.

Well, they'll be back, they'll pop up from their nap again. But after a while, they will learn to behave.

Wow. I think I just controlled something. I sent the fear-driven children away. I think I'm thinking a little more clearly now. What exactly did I do? Well first off I gave the noisy little toddlers of my fear-based emotions a name. I identified something and described it clearly. I saw how it was bothering me, not doing me any good, taking me away from the center of the triangle, which, by the way, I also thought my way into clearly articulating.

So what is within our power to control and what isn't?

When we form this question, we've landed right smack dab in the middle of Stoic philosophy, and we're putting it to work in or life. We're at the key entry point of our triangle, using our rational minds to observe not only the world around us but the world within us. It's within that world within us, of course, where we can exert significant measures of control. The world that exists apart from us may or may not conform to our wishes, mostly it won't happen in fact, but the world within us is where we truly live anyway. Remember the old adage—anytime I'm disturbed, the problem is within me.

And yet still the world around us runs wild, like a billion toddlers set loose to do exactly as they please it seems at times. Unfortunately, hardly any of them are my toddlers, who are happily napping right now. The analogy breaks down a little here. Lisa's boss, who didn't give her that promotion; Joseph's girlfriend who dumped him; Don's brother John, who may or may not see things as Don does, none of them are toddlers of course. Yet they all are forces that are out of the direct control of the people they're affecting, the unhappy protagonists of our three stories.

Yet they're all also people that must be reckoned with by our protagonists. Stoic principles, practiced daily, will help guide them in doing so. None any more so than, again, our favorite old adage, anytime something disturbs me, the problem is within me.

If we draw our boundaries carefully and clearly to just that point where we end, and the world begins, and strive to keep good order within our boundaries, our sense of well-being becomes not only untouchable; we begin to be able to experience love truly. We, at the very least, become most useful to those around us. Whether they see it or not, it is entirely beside the point. This isn't to say that we have the power to the right the world's wrongs. Let's be clear. We don't have that superpower. But we do contribute in positive and constructive ways that become a virtuous and self-reinforcing cycle both within us and in the world we live in. We strive to harmonize the two. Therein, say all the great sages, we begin to live.

Okay, so you're ready to sign up. That's great. First off, don't look for any thanks. So rather than that's great, let me rather say who cares as lesson number one. The world mostly doesn't care what your motivations are—why you've made a decision to practice Stoic principles in your daily life. Really, it just doesn't matter to anyone but you. Just like nobody's ill opinion of you should disturb you, neither should anyone's praise lift you up. Well, if you're married, there may be some minor, technical exceptions.

The point is if we're embarking on a program of self-mastery that results in a life of useful and harmonious well-being, and it's something you do because you want to because you've seen firsthand the futility of living a life based upon ego and self-centered motives.

It just hasn't worked out. Time and time again, you've run up against some brick wall or another. Or when you've won life's lotteries, gotten that great thing you thought was the answer to all your problems, you found out it wasn't all that great, that it failed to fill some deeper spiritual need. The fact is, day to day, life just isn't that great. It's all just a humdrum routine of mindless consumption, and nobody does I want them to do, and then it's all over.

Okay, let's start. Let's break away from all that.

Let's get free.

Chapter 6: The Stoic Way

Let's start with the basic concepts that are not only key Stoic ideas, but will form the basis of a weekly plan of meditation. These are all prominent in many of the world's great spiritual teachings.

Open-Mindedness

"There is a principle which is a bar against all information,

which is proof against all arguments and which cannot

fail to keep a man in everlasting ignorance -

that principle is contempt prior to investigation."

- Herbert Spencer

We're starting here not because it's the most important of Stoic virtues, but because without it, we're not going to get anywhere. A closed mind is, for all purposes, a dead mind. It's a mind which proclaims to the world. I know what I believe and require no further information. Please don't bother me. I've got it all figured out already. Thank you very much. It's the refuge of the lazy and the incurious. Eventually it becomes the indefensible fort of the intolerant, and finally just an isolating prison.

The ability to honestly take in information as it becomes available, as well as the ability to change one's opinions regarding any analysis which we conduct within the confines of our own minds, is a key and central tenet which all great Stoic practitioners acknowledge explicitly or implicitly. This I know, but tell me if you see it another way. Maybe I'm wrong. I'm ready for further reflection.

Remember that great observation of Heraclitus, Panta Rei, that everything is flowing. The world, particularly the world which we wish to live in, is in a constant transformational process that occurs in the present tense of every present moment. The past? Well, it's already over. The future? Very uncertain. Who knows what's going to happen?

To walk through life with an unchangeably fixed set of beliefs and attitudes, to experience life, in other words, with a closed mind, is to be a blind man without a cane, destined to trip up and get tangled in every kind of bramble and then deny it at the same time. It's not to have sight and not know it, to refuse a cane or helpful guide-dog or help of any kind. It's no kind of life at all. And yet we're all guilty of this over-attachment to views arrived at, whether by diligent asking and analysis, or views acquired from family. Nobody likes to be wrong.

Humility

Humility is a concept that's often confused with its cousin, humble. Or, even worse, carries connotations of obsequiousness or subservience. The best definition, for our purposes, is rather a state of being rightly related to the world. In the Stoic mind, if there's any subservience involved, it's subservience to reality and the truth. An excellent way of defining humility is the exact opposite of undue pride, which is one of fear's most prominent disguises.

Someone who lives in humility is a person living in concordance with the world around him, sure of his or her own status, and no more and no less than all others.

Also, for a truth-seeker, we can also see how making a conscious effort to practice humility is critical. In a world in which everything is in flux, where everything is flowing, won't truth itself be something ephemeral and inconstant? This is actually one of the big advances Stoicism makes from Platonic philosophy. Also, as a tool for a Stoic, who after all is a human being, prone to error, it guides away from the pride that can over-attach one to conclusions.

Honesty

If there is anyone cardinal virtue that stands out above others, it's certainly honesty. We place it here—third—after open-mindedness and humility since both are necessary tools to determine truth properly. How can I be honest, ascertain the truth, if my mind is closed? Or if I fail to practice humility? If I think somehow I'm a more superior person to my fellows, to those I encounter in the world around me, am I not blinding myself to what they may have to offer in the way of insight?

A Stoic's practice of rigorous and unblinking self-examination is the foundation of his or her practice. The success of his or her practice, and hence a sense of well-being, will be in direct proportion to the degree of commitment to the truth, no matter where it may lead, what uncomfortable conclusions it may sometimes lead to.

Fear and all its many guises of vanity, pride, and resentment, among others, require a constant and determined investigation to root out and identify. In time, this becomes almost second nature, however.

Acceptance

Acceptance inevitably runs a close second to honesty in a degree of critical importance for the Stoic practice. As we've already seen in our three examples, so much of life is out of our control, even though so many of our instinctive impulses lead us to try to shape all those events around us, particularly those that affect us immediately. The acceptance of reality as it is, not as we would like it to be, is not always easy. But haven't we seen the utter futility of our actions when we act, for some peculiar reason, as if we can imagine reality into being the way we'd like it to be? As if the world's reality will shape itself around our actions? We so often take this even to childish lengths; we use the magical thinking of children to picture the world we'd like to be.

Acceptance is the adult answer to so many of our problems and disturbances. For the Stoic, it's the beginning point of freedom, a quick and ready discernment, and then acceptance of reality provides the foundation for meaningful action.

Acceptance begins almost like a spiritual practice. Especially in regards to events where fear gains its best footholds, those events, such as death, affect us most deeply. In time, however, it becomes a quick response employed to determine the proper and right action to all manner of situations, large and small. One may struggle at first to find acceptance of life's most difficult occurrences, but in time you do because you must. There is no other alternative for a Stoic. Even if one has religious beliefs that involve a life after death, and there I will offer no argument against, I have no opinion or information on the subject, the fact remains that fear of death is primal and primary and affects us all.

I often think of Victor Frankl's experience in the Nazi concentration camp, in a situation where even the bravest among us might have wanted to give up and simply die, or gone mad due to the depth of the constant daily horror. Yet he found acceptance of what was surely one of the most terrible episodes in human history, survived and thrived.

Willingness

Willingness typically requires a preposition to take an easy and concrete definition. I'm willing to change, or willing to take out the garbage tonight, for instance, even though it's not my regular night to do so. To be willing is to be entirely ready to do something, which is really useful when, as a practicing Stoic, you determine a useful course of action, as you invariably will. And taking out the garbage when your partner's back is out is a pretty useful course of action. Just do it, and don't even tell him you did it. Don't look for any props or special thanks.

As a description of a general state of being, willingness is a little trickier. In fact, I would suggest as part of your Stoic practice of daily reflection and meditation, you think upon the concept. If you pray, then pray for willingness. If you meditate, think upon it long and hard. Being in a state of readiness is really being open to the world as it flows around you. Even though you control so very little of that flow, you're in it, part of it whether you like it or not. Stoicism isn't to shut off from the world, but more to rightly relate yourself to it. So relate to it and don't be afraid of it relating to you. Once you clearly set up and clearly perceive those boundaries, where you end, and the world begins, the boundaries become a place of remarkable transformation and joy. You're opening to life itself when you become clear who you are. The clear discernment of a boundary is, of course, a limitation. But it's also an indication where freedom begins.

So alongside all those things, we will find truly out of control, will also come unexpected opportunities to engage with the world. We're placing ourselves on a new and more solid foundation. And with all the old ego-driven fears melting away we'll be freer than ever before to engage the world in exciting and creative ways that would have never occurred to us before.

The World

We've been throwing around this term a lot, and it requires, at this point, a more precise definition. Let's first observe that it's everything that I'm not. Or for you, it's everything that you're not. And yet we're both in it as well. I know that's a little confusing but stay with me - we're not going to get lost down a metaphysical rabbit hole.

The Greeks, who first started practicing Stoicism back in that dusty farmer's market all those years ago, had a concept we'll call Phantasia. They used it to describe all the impressions that we receive in our minds from the world around us, that constant bombardment of sensory information the world sends our way or which registers in our minds as "the world." That would include you to me, or me to you, as we're hanging at the juice bar waiting for our drinks. It would also include the totality of everything else out there, well beyond the market, for each of us.

Yet as thinking beings, each of us is acutely aware of our self, that within this vast world, we exist as well. I'm a world existing within that greater world, registering the world as Phantasia, or let's just say impressions, which, as it all unfolds and flows along, is registering in my mind and shaping my very ability to perceive it. I'm both in it and somewhat apart from it.

It's precisely that knowledge of ourselves as part of and apart from that gives us the edge, makes us moral agents, able to exercise judgment. It's the ticket to freedom, why life is as much art as science. I'm an impression registering on my own mind too. Yet I'm in control of at least that one impression. Not so much, though, of the impression I'm making in your mind

The key point is where exactly does this ever-moving boundary between myself and the world occur? Where is it right now in this very moment in which I'm now, and you are too, right next to me, waiting on our juices? Yet I'm close enough to you, right now at least, to get a fairly good sense of the impression I'm making in your mind. Though I could be wrong, of course. I'm going to risk it, though, since you look a little sad, at least that's the impression I'm getting. I'm going to ask how you are. How's life treating you today? Then it's up to you how you respond. I don't have any control over that. But maybe we can be friends. I'd like that, though it's not something in my total control.

If you're a little standoffish, I'm not going to respond negatively in kind. I don't really know what's going on with you, what impression I or the world is really making. But I have decided that I wish well-being for you too. I can more easily arrive at this point because I'm a self-aware Stoic. And make my way through life with a clear understanding of myself and motives, and with the acceptance that the world is ever-shifting and full of others with, by definition, differing impressions.

Sound Stoic practice puts us squarely in the moment, where life is lived, not isolated and apart, but asking where the boundary is as it shapeshifts around. It puts us upon a plane where meaningful action can occur, an action that will keep us in the center of the triangle.

Self-Restraint

Going forward, let's just call this stepping back. A step back often precedes two steps forward as any good dancer can tell you. Let's admit right up front that nobody's going to do this Stoic deal perfectly. Those pesky little fear-driven emotions might, or will, actually, become more obedient in time, but they're always going to be around, waiting for a chance to cause mayhem and disrupt the flow of our tidy little triangle. That's their nature, I guess, and life would be pretty boring if everyone was some Buddha. Whatever would we talk about? How's perfect enlightenment today? It's good. How's perfect enlightenment with you? It's good. Okay, see you tomorrow.

Getting into the regular habit of pausing before speaking or acting in stressful situations will pay dividends well beyond perhaps anything else a Stoic does. It's the go-to tool in the box. How often have you regretted, even as the words were flowing into the text and you hit the send button, something you've just said. So why did you hit send? What were you hoping to accomplish? So often, we act in a rash and foolish way that not only defeat us in our immediate desire for well-being but harm those around us too. And people being people mostly don't forgive and forget. They retaliate. It may be today, or it may be tomorrow or even ten years from now, but you know they're coming for you. We've contributed to disharmony in general. That's not the side of the equation we want to be on.

Take a step back next time, at that moment of utterance or action. Especially, never write or speak in a state of disturbance. Or if you have to, keep it as simple as possible, the bare minimum of what is required. There are many exercises, a few we'll learn about in the following chapters, that will help make this a permanent feature of our daily life. In time, this practice of stepping back becomes reflexive. People won't even know you're doing it, although it's the moment you're giving to your mind to discern rationally what speech or act will keep you in the center of the triangle.

And then finally, there's mindfulness, which we'll use to describe all of the above. And will be a subject for constant meditation in the evening and throughout the day, a kind of shorthand that refers to the unity of all our concepts.

Mindfulness

We can best describe mindfulness as a general state of being, an attitude we strive to adopt in all our interactions with the world. It includes all of the above concepts, working in conjunction, and creating a whole and complete way of being more significant than the sum of all the parts. The practice of Stoic philosophy in our daily lives brings us to a higher state of consciousness. It is well-being in action as we navigate the shifting currents of each day, each year, each moment of our life.

Let's go back to our three examples and ask what similarities exist in our protagonists and the life situations they find themselves in.

First off, I'd observe that each of them hasn't clarified what's in the center of their triangle, so to speak. Or if they have, it's something guaranteed to lead them to recreate their unhappiness as they go on through life. I'd observe, in general, that they have probably not made the intellectual leap of separating eudaimonia, or well-being, from those various things they believe cause it, like a promotion, a relationship or an inheritance, money. All those things exist in that uncertain realm of the world, over which they have very little control. If I get the promotion, the girl or the boy, if I get the money, then I'll be happy.

They've signed over their lives, their sense of well-being, to forces out of their control. Our friends are confused; their motives are muddled, and they're doomed to repeat cycles of unhappiness and frustration. They strive to control events around them, and when events don't conform to their expectations, they respond with actions based upon reckless emotions animated, all of them, by fear. Meanwhile, precious days and years of their lives are passing them by.

Secondly, I'd observe that none of them have developed a daily program of reflection and meditation. And why should they? Despite the roiling morass of emotion, they find themselves in; the fact remains that, like for most of us who can afford to buy this book, all their basic animal needs of food and shelter are provided for. The modern world has given them, in fact, not only a previously unimagined standard of living but a constant and dizzying array of consumer choice in comfort and entertainment. Plus, the message that comes along with everything we seem to do or buy is this: You're the boss. You're number one. You're in total control here.

But really? If I'm so in charge, why I am so unhappy, so blah, so often? Stoicism, rather than an antique philosophical curiosity, actually provides real solutions to eternal human conundrums that seem to have only intensified in the modern world.

The world seems to point us away from humility, contentment, and well-being. Why is that? Is it as simple that a person self-contained, living in well-being, and in harmony with the world, just needs a lot less stuff? I'm going to let you answer that one.

Breaking away from old patterns of behavior isn't easy. Change never is. That's a message we tend to wish not to hear. The basic ideas of Stoicism, which are spiritual in nature, are perhaps in conflict with the smooth running of a vast consumption-based economy, required to grow and expand, and which seems based upon the stimulation and gratification of primal desires. Stoicism tells us that true ease and comfort, true well-being, requires no further purchases. But it does require effort.

Chapter 7: The Stoic's Daily Regimen

When opening your eyes first from sleep, as your mind moves away from sleep and into consciousness of yourself and of the day, take a brief moment to express gratitude, even if perhaps you don't feel it, even if you're cranky before that first cup of coffee, repeat some such words of gratitude as "I'm thankful for this gift of my life and the gift of this day."

This is particularly important to do when you "don't feel like it." You're not dishonest. You've made a decision to place well-being at the forefront. You've moved away from the world of so-called "feeling good" as the basis for your life. Also, in doing so, we place our rational mind into the forefront, as well as implicitly acknowledge we have well-being as our central goal. And it only takes a moment.

Set aside time in the morning routine for meditation. Thirty, fifteen, even ten minutes will do. But whatever it is, stick to it. The establishment and the maintenance of a daily routine are just as important as the subject of your meditation. We're looking to build new habits that will constantly reinforce and create new attitudes within us and hence in our relations with the world. Explicit reflection upon each of the seven concepts will be the means through which we bring them into active use in our daily lives.

For the first few weeks or months here are specific meditations you can use to get started. After a time, you may find others that work better for you. Most important is that we keep to our routine, whatever the time allotted is.

Half of each morning's routine, in the beginning, should consist of specific contemplation and exercises as follows:

Monday Morning – Open-Mindedness

Imagine yourself walking in a field. It's a beautiful day, and you're comfortable and at ease. You come upon a large flower. Imagine its details, its color, the shapes of the petals. Imagine your mind as a flower that opens to the warmth of the sun. See it closing and then in the process of opening. Repeat this several times, relax into the image. Then envision the idea of truth as something that settles into the flower, perhaps a bee or a bird into the flower as it closes, and then see it leave as it reopens.

Now reflect upon your mind alone. Imagine it as a large boulder. Put your hands on the boulder; feel it.

Ask yourself, which am I? Think literally about open-mindedness. What's the dictionary definition? Recall instances in your life and try to identify specific moments when you've been receptive to a new idea, a new impression, a new person, and times when you haven't.

Tuesday Morning – Humility

Reflect on pride first. Think of specific instances when you've said or done things that have disturbed you, when you've acted selfishly and regretted it. Try to isolate what was threatened in you. Was it your pride? You assumed that someone was judging you in a negative way. Odds are if often was pride.

Now imagine the event again but with how you would have liked to have acted, or said what you wished you had said. Maybe it was something in your childhood, maybe something the day before. Say to yourself, when a similar situation arises in my life, and it will, this is how I'll respond.

Think deeply about the word humility. Imagine it as water.

Wednesday Morning – Honesty

Imagine an awesome scene of natural beauty, some place that has moved you in the past. A sunset, a mountain view, an ocean view perhaps. Let yourself wander into it and explore. Imagine the sounds. Take time doing this, immerse yourself.

Then ask yourself, why does this move me? Try to isolate the sense of awe, and then separate it from the scene, and then watch your scene fall away while holding onto the sense of grandeur imagining it materialize as something coming into your hands. You can feel it, give it the shape and weight you wish. Say this is the truth, this grandeur, the scene was merely the messenger. It is to this I dedicate myself. This is the truth, and it is present in all things, in all moments. Now imagine it in your hands changing into something with a different texture and weight.

Repeat this several times with different scenes.

Thursday Morning – Acceptance

Reflect upon the serenity prayer. Say it as a prayer if you'd like first. Grant me the serenity to accept things I cannot change, courage to change things I can, wisdom to know the difference.

Isolate each clause and reflect upon it independently. What are the things I can't change? Imagine all the impressions the world made upon you the previous day. Which among them did you have the power to change? And it what ways might you have tried? Reflect upon moments when you specifically tried to effect change, perhaps when maybe you paused a moment and rethought something you were about to blurt out. Or maybe even some dessert you passed on. Or some spiritual exercise you did. Now recall your response afterward, the sense of well-being that flowed from it. Bring back to your mind the moment of decision when you turned away from the ill-advised thing. Say this was wisdom in action.

Now imagine the totality of the world. Draw as large a picture as you can of the universe. Then place yourself as small as possible in relation to your mind's picture—express acceptance of this.

Now remove yourself from the picture—express acceptance of this.

Friday Morning – Willingness

Imagine yourself moving with a river flowing through a landscape. You can imagine the landscape as a scene of nature, or an urban scene, or even something very familiar as a route you take to work every day, but there's no destination, you're going right past your job, it's moving along, and you're moving through it in the water. Take some time and enjoy the scene and the sense of flowing with it, then say this is a willingness, I'm ready to go wherever the flow wishes.

Now reflect upon the concept of willingness, giving it the preposition of "to" and ask yourself what you are willing to follow. What is the flow of the river?

Saturday Morning – The World

Imagine a busy intersection in a busy city or town. Place yourself in the middle, standing safely on the sidewalk perhaps. A bustle of cars and people are around you. Imagine it as completely as you can. Now keep yourself there and detach another part of yourself, rise up and float over the scene, seeing yourself on the sidewalk in the middle of the bustle, pause for a moment.

Then continue on rising until you're above the entire city or town until you can see the countryside and suburbs appear. Use your specific city if it helps, a place you know. But continue rising until you can see your region and then country and then the entire disc of the planet receding away from you, the disc becoming smaller and smaller, marble size, then a dot and until finally, it's just another point of light.

Now reverse your motion and return. Watch the world come back to marble size. It's blue and becoming larger again, disc-sized again, then the shape of your country, region and city return and you continue until you're again right over the intersection where you're still standing, and pause. Then come back into yourself and see the busy scene from that safe place on the sidewalk.

Someone is standing next to you. Ask them how they're doing today. It is Saturday. You've got the day off, tell them.

Sunday Morning – Self-Restraint

Imagine yourself in on a busy highway somewhere, and you're driving along, with a purpose. You need to get somewhere fast, your exit is coming up but then all of a sudden, inexplicably, traffic freezes. Your exit is just a few car lengths ahead, and maybe you can squeeze through but all of a sudden someone pulls alongside you, honks your horn, indicates they'd like to get in front, take that tight space that can get them off the freeway.

Wave them on.

They squeeze through, but suddenly another car pulls up and wants to get through.

Wave them on.

Continue this and try to recall how frustrated you've been in such situations before.

Wave another one on.

Get to that point of utter frustration that precedes a middle finger extended, say, or some rash thing said or done.

Wave another one on.

Now imagine yourself decompressing, moving from frustration to something pleasing.

Wave another one on.

Repeat.

Wave on at least twenty more cars, or until you've reached utter contentment.

Okay, so for the other half of our morning routine we turn our thought to the day before us, and we do this every morning. What situations are coming down the pike? Is there anything we're especially anxious about? If so, we imagine that situation, ourselves in the middle of it, what do we want to achieve. And then we say to ourselves, "I'm ready to accept how this situation resolves itself or plays out no matter what."

We do not do this while we're gulping down our second cup of coffee, cramming a bagel down. We've set aside this time each and every morning, in a quiet and peaceful setting, to be alone with our thoughts. We're practicing Stoics.

We imagine the absolute worst possible outcome, and we say to ourselves if this is the way it is to be I will accept it. We remind ourselves that this day is a precious gift, but that not everything will occur as I hope it will and I accept in advance whatever it is that does occur. Furthermore, regardless of the outcomes of any event I participate in, I will strive to practice all the virtues upon which I meditate. I will maintain a demeanor of peace, even if, particularly if, feelings of frustration appear.

Think in a more general way now about the uncertainty of the future and the worth of being present in the present tense of every present moment, where life occurs. Say to yourself that when something unfortunate happens, I'll strive first to step back and see it for what it is, then see what opportunity it provides for me to be of use to someone else.

Most others we encounter probably don't have a program of spiritual development, but of course, maybe they do. Regardless, it's of no concern to us. We prepare our self to enter the day with a sense of gratitude and willingness to be of use to others around us, expecting no thanks or praise in return. We're secure in our knowledge that our own well-being in no way derives from any external force around us.

All Throughout the Day

As we go through our day, our practice of Stoic virtues continues. See every moment as a chance to use them, both when challenged by difficult events and when pleased by events. Don't put stock in those moments when in fact we seem to achieve some worldly goal, for then we're placing our reliance on ephemeral events. When something does occur that would lead you to say, great, I got that raise, for instance, exercise humility, remind yourself the feelings that would have tried to upset you had it not happened. In this way, we strengthen the smooth flowing of our triangle, our emotions stay in proper relation to our mind and our actions, our behavior.

When this fails, as it will, at times, tell yourself that the problem rests entirely within yourself. Hopefully, you've limited the damage by stepping back from a challenging situation, but even if you haven't, don't do further damage by lapsing into undue regret or self-recrimination. This is pointless and further disharmonizes the world. Rather, take time out to analyze whatever it was that just occurred. Seek to honestly root out what part you may have played in the disturbance so that you can learn from it. If you determine the true nature of the matter, and specifically if you were at fault in some way, see it as a chance to make amends by a heartfelt apology to someone, as well as an opportunity to grow in your practice.

When dealing with somebody who seems hostile to you, try to understand first that you have no direct control over what they say or do. Also, most importantly, you have no way of surely assessing their motive. First, you step back from the situation. You can say to yourself, this person is my brother or sister, yet I don't know what it is that is truly bothering them, nor do I even need to know. I wish them well. Go in peace. Say this and mean it truly and you will be well on your way to much contentment.

Contemplate instead what is good about both your apparent enemies as well as your friends. Try to put yourself in every other's place, but without motives of disregard or making yourself superior to them. See them as fellow human beings who may or may not be living with the benefit of a clearly developed understanding of the world. Err always on the side of the most generous opinion of others, especially those who challenge your sense of well-being. Instead of retaliation think in terms of usefulness to others.

Think often about the ephemeral and impermanent nature of the world and all those in it, most particularly yourself. Everything comes into being for only a moment before it changes into something else, including ourselves. View everything as a gift so that when you no longer have it, that Tesla is a fine car for sure, there is no remorse. All things are eventually given back and become the stuff of further gifts. In this way, we enter into and even extend further harmony in our ever-flowing world.

And indeed always strive to imagine yourself as part of the entire universe, a small part, to be sure, but a part nevertheless. This is the truest satisfaction, our very deepest need, to be a part of the great universe. Everything is part of everything else, part of some whole which we all carry with us. We're all fellow travelers, and there's no small satisfaction to be wrested from that knowledge. People will never do as our primitive emotions would have them do. For that matter, neither will they behave as we would have them behave when we have what we think our best selves can imagine is in their best interests. The universe isn't so arranged, and perhaps there's some great plan in that.

Again, one of the great practitioners of Stoic philosophy and principles, Marcus Aurelius, was no less an Emperor of Rome at the height of its powers. Rarely in history has such undiluted power rested in one single individual. And yet he himself, even as he set policy that impacted literally millions of people all over the Roman Empire, even as he sent Roman Legions off to countless provinces to enforce those policies in quite coercive ways, he was able to correctly identify the futility of an individual's attempts to control not only the future but often the simplest events in which he may find himself. In the end, what universe we might control exists within ourselves. Think often about that.

In the Evening Before Bed

Before we go to sleep, we take a similar amount of time to pause, reflect, and meditate.

We think about the entirety of the day's events, how we anticipated them in the morning, how they differed, what in fact occurred. What stood out, particularly? In what ways did we succeed in putting our principles in action? In what way did we fail? When were we falling into disturbance and confusion? What were the exact circumstances? How did I do well, and how did I come up short.

Did I exercise humility, or did pride get the best of me? Look specifically at the instances, examine things you may have said or omitted saying. In what ways was pride a factor? And why? What was threatened by you?

Was I honest with those around me, most particularly was I honest with myself? Or did I tell some lies, large or small? Did I truly fail to reckon with something to myself?

Did I find acceptance of particular circumstances which at other times might have disturbed me? If so, what exactly happened? What did you do differently? Or did I attempt to determine an outcome of some event over which I had no influence? Who got invited to the company Christmas party perhaps. Or did something just not go my way and I acted like a baby? The line at Starbucks was so long I had to settle on office coffee, made me snap at my coworker smugly sipping her latte. Yes, get into the small details. It's often in them that our true motives get revealed and growth happens. People can be pretty petty, and there are few exceptions, but you're going to be getting better but looking at them closely. It's not going to be every day that large events occur. And you didn't even know it was the coffee that set you off until you got into it a little.

Where was I simply generous and kind for no reason at all? Ask yourself this every night. If the answer is at no point at all, don't worry. If you ask yourself this question repeatedly, every single night, odds are good that you'll start to answer it positively. Tomorrow will be full of opportunities.

We do this not to punish ourselves or even reward ourselves, but merely as a kind of fact-finding mission conducted in a mood of calm repose. We hope to benefit from our experience, see where we might improve, see where we have improved. We're on the path though, pointed in the direction of the center of the triangle.

Most importantly, like with our morning meditations, we do this regularly and without exception. The time we take in both the morning and in the evening is the central fact of our lives as practicing Stoics. Without a strict regime of reflection and self-examination, we accomplish nothing; we might as well just go back to our old ways, crawl back into the prison cells of our minds and lives, lock the door and throw away the key. I hear there's a good teenage slasher comedy superhero movie on FX. And just go for that half-gallon of ice cream in the freezer while you're at it. Eat the whole thing. Chase it down with a fifth of Scotch, too.

Or maybe you can have a little bit of each if you have to. But do your program first at least. Let's get honest at this moment. A comfortable bed awaits us, along with another wonderful opportunity at life tomorrow.

And finally, let's take this moment also to express some gratitude for the wonderful gifts we've been given. Let's recount what's really important, whatever that might be for you. I'm sure you can think of something. I usually end with thanks for the gift of my life.

Chapter 8: Championship Stoicism

Okay, the idea of championship-level Stoicism is a little bit of joke, but not entirely. Stoic principles can be practiced in many ways and degrees of depth. Here, we've really only made the barest of beginnings. But that's how everything good, lasting and worthwhile begins of course. This chapter is going to present a wide range of Stoic practice, beliefs, and exercises, many of them from current practitioners today. We'll suggest ways you can continue, deepen and strengthen your practice of Stoic principles, take it to that championship level and get up there with Epictetus and Aurelius.

Practice, Practice, Practice

It's sometimes said that there are people that do. And then there are people who think.

The man of action is decisive and goes out and conquers things, starts a great enterprise, or maybe becomes a really great baseball player but isn't someone really that interesting to talk with. "We had a great game today." Or, "Sometimes it just doesn't go your way." I'd observe that's about all I ever hear in every super insightful postgame interview.

And then there's those who sit around and think all day. Or they look at their belly button and meditate on that. Or just channel surf all day. Then maybe write a book occasionally that tells others how to think, about the nature of their belly button, or how to be a great channel surfer.

The Stoic idea says that one should do both, but that the order is what's crucial. The thought is useful and purposeful when it precedes action. Action is often meaningless without thought. How much time do we waste in going over the negative results of actions taken that were not deliberative? Like the folks in our three examples, we end up creating further confusion within ourselves and in those around us. Or how often do we take actions that prove fruitless and disruptive, for not being based upon a clear understanding of ourselves, our most basic values or goals?

Yet the flow isn't always one way. It's also true that it's from an honest examination of our experience that we can gain knowledge. The mind, when we meditate particularly, apparently has a clever directional device that gets to reverse the flow. I'm really glad the mind is in control.

The Stoic strives to base action upon self-knowledge and prior reflection, but also to learn and base our knowledge upon our experience. Again, it's all a flow. One common thread, though, is that this takes practice, practice and more practice. It's a daily undertaking.

"We (Stoics) warn not to be satisfied with thinking by itself. Add practice and training. As time goes on, we can forget what we learned.

We can then often end up doing the opposite."

- Epictetus

Not only do you improve when you do something often. When applied to matters of the mind, it also reinforces the concepts that underpin what it is you're doing. All great athletes know this, of course. I love baseball players, by the way, and a few of them are quite insightful regarding the nature of their beautiful game. Our point is to find the happiest flow between the rational faculties of our mind and the body and actions through which we express our self to the world, and through which we receive impressions of the world.

This takes daily practice. Nobody becomes good at what they do without, first, a clear understanding of the intent, and second, a determined effort to further sharpen those skills upon which we are able to achieve the goal.

Acquainting oneself with the Stoic principles in this book isn't the same as making an effort to make them work in your life. This requires a concerted effort. You've read and thought. Hopefully, you'll continue to read and think. But now it's time to start practicing, to develop a practice.

What is practice anyway? Is it something like what a doctor does, or any professional for that matter? It certainly is. A doctor, or a lawyer, has a practice. The word practice here is a noun. It describes a thing. Over time the doctor has perhaps a thousand patients who see her on a regular basis. The attorney has the same, customers, an office, perhaps, a place of business. They both have practices, which are distinct and individual things, nouns.

They've also practiced quite a lot to achieve them. Here, the word is a verb, to practice. It describes, as all verbs do, an action. They've studied extensively in school. They came to master certain aspects of their fields of study, medicine, and law. They've practiced (action, verb) their way to rewarding practices (thing, noun).

The more you practice, the better and more rewarding your practice of Stoicism will be. If you don't practice, then forget about having a practice, and all its rewards. A Stoic doesn't sit around and think all day. Stoic practices and has practice. The Stoic ideal is both noun and verb. The Stoic ideal merges action and thought to create a way of living life.

The Ideal Stoic Practitioner

Modern Stoics, like many of the Ancient Stoics, suggest that it's useful to develop a concept of an ideal practitioner. You should do so as well. Oftentimes, in the course of the day, you'll be presented with those step-back moments of pause, when a difficult situation or difficult emotions present themselves. Or in your reflection at night upon events already occurred, you'll wonder what the correct course of action was, or should have been.

It's helpful to formulate an ideal Stoic. For many modern Stoics, this is an actual person from history, such as Epictetus, or that Roman Emperor, Marcus Aurelius. Or it could even be someone you invent, maybe an ideal version of you, the perfect Stoic. Some modern Stoics claim to use comic book heroes such as Batman or Superman, who were both infallible and invincible Stoics in many ways.

So when that moment appears, and it will, part of you can easily refer to that ideal figure. You can ask yourself what would Superman, Wonder Woman, or Marcus Aurelius do in this situation? As Seneca observed, "Without a ruler, how can we draw a straight line?" To create a picture of an ideal Stoic ruler in your mind, attribute to that figure all the Stoic knowledge you'll be accumulating. So that when difficult situations occur, you'll have a quick and ready reference point, a ruler to help you draw the straight line to correct action.

Always Practice Mindfulness

We've already suggested that mindfulness can be thought of as the sum total of all your Stoic knowledge, or practice. It's becoming who you are, but it's also something distinct. It is that part of you that is constantly striving to put Stoic principles at work in all the situations of life, those grave and those routine ones as well. You're identifying yourself as a basically rational human being. Or at least that's the part of you in charge of your behavior.

You value above all else wisdom and virtue, Of this doesn't mean that you're always on you guard, or living in a fearful state. Rather, share yourself freely with all those around you. You're being guided by core principles now, and you might find that those other people will actually seek out your company because they enjoy being around you. But, then again, maybe not. You're not in control of that.

Bring your yourself back often to your actions in the here and now, regardless. When you're in the world, busy with tasks and such, perhaps imagine that you're the captain of a ship you've just left, a ship that's anchored in a harbor within your sight. You're on leave and enjoying the freedoms of a day onshore. But you're still the captain of that ship just offshore and could be called back at any moment, to take charge of a difficult situation.

In time, this will become second nature. The ship, where all the tools and resources you've gathering from your practice of Stoic principles, will become a certainty so basic that the trip back aboard becomes your second nature. It becomes the most useful and basic part of yourself. It becomes who you are.

Again, this doesn't happen without the concerted effort of daily practice. Like anything else, the more you do it, the less you're even aware you're doing. You're gaining mastery with each day spent in pursuit of goals, backed by the regimen you follow without fail, every morning and night, and all through the day. Mindfulness doesn't prevent from being fully part of the world. It doesn't stop you from being a great dad, a cherished spouse, an esteemed colleague. Indeed, none of these things are even your rock bottom goals. They all just tend to happen when you allow Stoic principles to guide your life.

Forgiveness or Detachment

"When someone acts or speaks falsely, know that he is acting

in ignorance. Know that nobody truly acts badly when

they possess true understanding. It seemed to that person

they were acting correctly at that moment."

- Epictetus

This is surely one of the toughest lessons. But the Stoics believed that everybody speaks and acts as if what they're doing is right the moment when they're doing it. Is this a patently untrue statement? Perhaps. But look a little more closely at it. There are two important observations we should make. First, is the idea that not everybody has the benefit, or perhaps even the capacity, of a rigorous program that aims to bring them to truth and true self-knowledge. They're living in ignorance.

I would take this one step further and observe, based upon Stoic philosophy and principles, that even my own self-knowledge is limited and imperfect. Who am I to judge another? Sometimes it's best to just step back from a person or situation for good, not in defeat but with a sense of neutrality. I just don't know. I surrender. It will certainly be most often the case that any remedy is outside of my control, and I need to accept whatever the circumstance or person is.

Secondly, is that idea of "in the moment." People tend to act, particularly in the moments of stressful urgency, when perhaps they're under undue influence from their own fear-drive egos as if what they're doing is right. They think they're right, at that moment, even while ten seconds later they're full of immediate regret, so destabilizing are the forces unleashed by emotions under perceived threat. The Stoic recognizes this, how reality is shaped and often quite warped in moments of high emotion and spends considerable energy addressing this problem.

So we should also always ready our self to take a posture of pity or forgiveness for others who, just like us, can act in unfortunate ways under the stress of threat and high emotion. Or be ready to practice that step back of detachment at the very least. Retaliating in kind serves as no kind of lesson to those we think are wrong, and it certainly doesn't help us.

So I should always turn the other cheek? No, not exactly. But anger that can be born from these situations will not only further inflame and lead to further immediate negative consequences, but it will also threaten to continue wreaking havoc within ourselves in the form of resentment. It is upsetting the flow of our life and taking us out of our sense of well-being. Will you give anyone or anything that power? Remember, any time I'm disturbed the problem is within me.

And resentments are like cancers that invade our bodies and minds. They're agents of fear, irrational and childish fear. Resentment can cause so much energy to be wasted, going over and over again whatever the specific imagined fault or event might be. In its wake come self-righteous anger, and then self-pity, and then, always, that smoldering desire to get even, to strike back. We go back to that moment, relive it again but with a version in which we come out victorious. Resentments truly are a disruption to our peaceful flow, but also a kind of flowing in themselves, turbulence of its own debilitating kind.

The word resentment is formed from the Latin verb sentire, which is to feel. When we suffer resentment, we're re-feeling something, something intolerable to us which prevents us any sense of repose or calm. And we then re-feel it again, as if going back through the particulars we'll be able to cure the disturbance within by giving it some other ending, perhaps, or imagining our self as some kind of virtuous hero figure who, this time, is able to vanquish the offender, coming out victorious. Or perhaps we simply wallow in self-pity, casting our self as a victim, perversely enjoying and basking in the implied sense of rightness that the imagined wrong is done to us reveals.

How seldom do we simply detach and take a look? Our ego-driven, outraged self won't permit it, so fierce is its hold upon us. But we must. We must step back and look at it clearly and determine our part in the disturbance if we've let it proceed to that point. When we do so, do we not often find that in some way we've made essential contributions to the disturbance? What did we say, for instance? Did it serve to inflame further? Or did we omit something? Did something we failed to contribute to the remonstration we suffered and which disturbed us? Was their some version of the dog ate my homework we used to explain why we didn't do something we should have done?

Best of all, it's much easier to walk away when confronted by those who would do us harm in this way. Particularly when it's clear that only a kind of defeat can result from impulsive engagement with whatever might be the source of the potential disturbance.

Finally, the Stoic principle is that the true fault is within us when we're disturbed by any and all things. It's a failure of humility and a failure of acceptance. We should often think about this. The world and its seemingly endless ability to wound us is just that—it's apart from us, it's the world, not me.

Before sleep, this should be the very first order of reflection, if such disturbances have occurred in the day. We detach and apply honest effort to review those events that have disturbed us. We inquire with an open and willing heart their true nature. Now, this is key. We do this without any intention of righting them, but only with the intention of learning from them. We detach completely and analyze, paying particular attention to our own wrongs, if any, in the situation. But it's almost certain that if we are disturbed, we will have played some negative role in the event, however great or small that role may have been. Indeed, it's crucial that we isolate the exact particulars of our role. Once we've done this to our satisfaction, we make a firm resolve to not only correct our behavior in future instances, but most importantly to set right any wrong we may have committed, and to do so at the earliest opportunity. Even if we feel like our wrong is minor compared to the imagined wrong we suffered

If this is something that can be accomplished the next day, we do it then, or even immediately, if possible. We make no delay, whatever the specific circumstance. We make amends without any thought of any perceived wrong we may have suffered. We go to the person and acknowledge the exact harm frankly, sparing no detail. For instance, we might say to a coworker we squabbled with, "Yesterday I said ….. and I called you …..and that was wrong of me to say those things." Then, with true Stoic humility, we ask what we can do to make the situation right, and we listen to any response with an open mind and heart.

Sometimes this may lead to a reciprocal admission of wrongdoing, or it may not. It's out of your control how another response. If the admission of wrongdoing, on your part, was done honestly and without recrimination, the result will be purifying for you, and that's the point. While we don't control the world and all those others around us, we are responsible for our own conduct. When we undertake such amends correctly, whatever resentment is tormenting us regarding the matter will simply fall away. We've done what we could do to make an unfortunate situation right. Again, best of all, we use all those tools at our disposal, upon which we base our morning meditations, to never allow such situations to arise in the first place. But they occasionally will for us all, most likely. But they'll happen less and less as we progress.

Self-Deprivation

Let's now talk about something you may have noticed we haven't spoken much about. That's the idea that Stoicism is often associated with notions of self-deprivation. All we can say is that it is an entirely correct observation, that it has been and still is for many. Many Stoic practitioners see the exercise of depriving themselves of certain bodily comforts as central to their practice of Stoic principles. There are, of course, other Stoic practitioners who think and practice differently, who leave the rigor for their internal practice. I believe the sensible thing is to leave it entirely up to each and every person, that no purity test should be involved in claiming the mantle of

Stoicism. The judgment of others, after all, is something Stoics try to steer away from.

That said, I do recommend you give it a try. In a sense, if you go to the gym or otherwise work-out, or even eat a sensible diet that steers you away from all the empty calories your primitive mind is telling you are super tasty, you're already practicing a little self-deprivation. I'd say keep an open mind and at least try to ramp it up a few notches, make it into a purely spiritual exercise. The modern world assaults us with so many messages about ease and comfort, about 'feeling-good' in that very primitive way of satisfying the most base appetites, it feels even a little revolutionary just to say screw ease and comfort, I'm roughing it today. It's a small way of taking some control, sticking it to the man even, but the kind of control that can, and I can reinforce some of our basic principles of meaningful Stoic living.

It can be as simple as taking a cold shower this morning. That's a pretty obvious one, for sure. But let me tell you, first thing in the morning when you turn the spray of water too cold only, and I mean cold, and face it before you interject your body into it, it's easier said than done. But do it anyway. Remember, you've got an open mind now. Just try it. Get in there and, owwwwwwwwwwww, man you are so awake right now! Grab that soap and shampoo and get clean because all of a sudden, you are so very and extremely awake!

Afterward, as you're drying off, you might even notice you like it. It's something new. The world seems a little different. You probably don't need that second cup of coffee.

Or try simplifying your diet on a regular basis. I mean not just eat healthfully—I hope you're doing that anyway—but leave off sweets entirely for a week. That favorite thing you like on the weekends? Deliberately substitute a bland alternative sometimes.

There's a sense in which these deprivations became a gratitude exercise. They make us keenly aware of the things we enjoy when they're absent. Also, we're training our mind to reject over-reliance on comforts, and we're keeping the toddlers at bay, still taking that nap.

Self-deprivation can also be seen as a ritual enactment of those things we're trying to accomplish in our minds, which, after all, are trapped in our bodies. It's an acknowledgment similar to how a Stoic acknowledges death and other unfortunate facts of life. The body is just as finite we are. Its desire for ease and comfort, for paths of least resistance, however, can and do have a corrupting influence on our rational faculties. We can transcend our fears of death by acknowledging it frankly as a fact.

We can transcend and gain mastery over our minds by taking mastery over our bodies, its insistence that we behave according to its wants and desires, those wants and desires which we've seen are also quite childish, and so often lead us to foolish behavior.

The list of little pleasures that we can and perhaps should deny ourselves as part of the Stoic practice is long. The good news, certainly what I've found, is that after embarking upon my Stoic practice, the desire for all those little comforts and distractions tend to fall away of their own accord. They find their proper place. I'm more settled and need less and less to reach outside myself for relief. My relief is more and more entirely from within. That said, I do recommend experimenting with other forms of self-denial.

Particularly, the constant reach to the phone when you're uncomfortable or bored is perhaps a good place to start. That impulse to check the sugar rush of a new like or follower, the latest news story. Ask yourself, instead, what is it in this present moment causing me discomfort? Or is it just a reflex? Why is so much of my sense of well-being tied up into all those messages I'm getting from it? It's in our uniquely modern dependence upon electronic devices that so much of our unhappiness derives and is expressed, contributing to destabilizing flowing both within us and from without us.

Take regular digital vacations! Or just take the damn phone and flush it down the toilet, even better! Lead the way into the digital free future! Friend, I'm right behind you!

Or at the very least, moderate your use.

Moderation

The idea of self-deprivation leads us nicely into the topic of moderation. As I've just suggested, pursuing an active practice of Stoic principles tends to, in and of itself, lead us into happy moderation. We suddenly feel less and less the impulse to reach outside of our self to keep in the middle of the triangle. It just happens. Feelings of purpose and self-esteem flow into our daily lives. We've put our self into a new relation to the world around us. It's a self-reinforcing cycle too. Those around us begin to become stabilizing forces as well, they're responding to the changes within us and in turn, contribute to the stability. We're no longer fighting them so much, getting tangled up in emotionally charged messes with those closest to us. Of course, this isn't always the case. But we're stepping back when agitated, thinking clearly before acting, we're staunching the wounds, at the very least.

We're beginning to live lives of thoughtful moderation. And we can and should make a conscious effort to deepen this naturally occurring trend. It's where we connect most deeply with life as it flows around and through us, our self-centered egotism continues slipping away further and further as we further embrace moderation as a virtue.

All things in moderation are probably one of those ideas nobody can disagree with. But let's be clear that we're not proselytizers. The choices that others make in matters of personal conduct are really no business of our own. We can only serve as examples, humble examples, for others through the example of our life as we lead it. This is entirely within our power.

Choose, therefore, to exercise restraint and moderation in all areas of life. Of course, sometimes you have to let your hair down and go out and have some crazy fun too. To deny oneself fun at all times kind of sounds like a bummer sounds actually downright immoderate. So when you do break your fast, make it count and really live it up, and then get right back to the program.

Memento Mori

You're going to die. Damn. Really? Yes. Meditate on this great fact often.

Surely there's no greater instinct within us than that primal urge we're given to avoid all manner of situations in which we may meet an untimely demise. Our mind is hard-wired in every way possible to avoid death. Avoidance of death is also the essential heartbeat of fear. It's the great free pass which fear has and allows it entry into everything we do and everything we think. This is actually quite useful. One can even say that here fear makes itself into our best buddy, looking out for us and we should be quite grateful we have such a friend.

The problem, of course, is that fear rarely attends just to its primary responsibility. In conjunction with our amazing capacities to imagine the world in all its dazzling complexity, fear is often still there, sneaking around, causing all kinds of havoc in the form of pride, greed, vanity, among many other disguises.

We'll never "conquer" fear. The idea is really quite absurd. But we can get fear to behave more reasonably, get it back into its lane so it can do its job.

Meditating, often upon the subject, helps puts fear into its proper place. This isn't a morose exercise, but a simple acceptance of the fact that it helps us live on the plane of reality. Our death will, in fact, will be timely, we just don't know when that time is, it's out of our control. When we come to an acceptance of this fact we become free to live, we become most deeply aware of how precious this life we have is, we're tuned into the marvelous wonders and mysteries of life's flow, we're able to live our deepest and most meaningful life. We live each and every day as if it were a complete life in itself.

Let Go of What Other People Think about You

Reputations are important, right? Especially if you're career-minded. It's important that people think you're capable, able to do the job, particularly that next job you're aiming for.

A Stoic approach to this is clear. What others think of us, the opinions they may hold regarding any matter, are entirely out of our control. The cost of giving credence to others' opinions of us is high. We take our sense of well-being out of our own hands and give into the hands of those we have no control of. Ancient Stoics have observed that being concerned with praise, or seeking the warm glow of approval from others, is an unsound basis for any action. We do something because it is the right thing to do.

Action-based upon the seeking of praise is clearly action guided by our self-centered egotism. Perhaps even more to the point, it's absurd. We have no way of even knowing what people "expect" us to be, which is an absurd notion as well. Of course, in a workplace, or at home, we have certain duties and obligations, and we perform them well, not because we'll receive praise for doing so, but because there is satisfaction in and of itself, and to not perform duties would lead to unhappiness.

And what a suffocating mantle it is as well, to be always worrying about some opinion someone else may or may not have of you. In this regard, Stoicism leads to easy and immediate benefits. We free our self from vanity, and the fear-driven egotism is driving it. But it no way does this give license to act in ways that do harm to others, to say the 'brutally honest' or insensitive thing that could disturb another. Rather, this constant monitoring of how we appear, the 'impression' we're making, falls off like a suffocating coat on a warm day.

But neither do we hold back from sharing our self, particularly with our family and friends. It's false that Stoics are emotional robots of some kind. When we share ourselves with others, we're participating in life, giving, and receiving. Freed from undue concern over how we appear to anyone, we're suddenly freer to act truly in the interest of everyone. Our motives are clear.

Make Clear Goals but Don't Obsess over Results

We've spent a lot of time discussing the idea of control. We've concluded that we're not in control of a whole lot that exists around us. We live in the world, but we don't run the world, far from it. Every time we act as if we do, we seem to get jammed up. Nobody really does run the world. I personally think that's a good thing.

And yet we live in the world. We need to have a job or earn money in some way. We have to cooperate with others to do so. Marriage, friendship, raising kids are all central aspects of life from which great meaning and joy are derived, but are also the source of our deepest conflicts and pain. We are deeply social creatures. Recognizing that you're not calling the shots doesn't mean that not you're in a competitive world where you want to carve out a place for yourself. And that nobody's going to give it to you for nothing.

We've determined that our clearest goal, the center of our triangle, is well-being. This typically includes our desire that those we love have well-being as well, and that it's all part of a happily self-reinforcing triangle of well-being. Happy wife, happy life, and I can't think of anything that rhymes with husband, but it's all very gender-neutral.

But surely we have more specific goals as well. There's nothing in Stoic practice that should keep you from articulating and working towards the achievement of such goals, whatever they may be. Goals come with expectations; of course, they project into the future. And this is where your Stoic practice comes into play. Things we hope for, in the future, often don't turn out the way we wish them to. And in the projection of our minds into the future, with all its uncertainties, our Stoic program of calm, useful repose can crumble and take us right back where we started, in a mess, unhappy, not living in the present tense of the present moment.

It's as much art as science, this Stoic deal. The state of Stoic mindfulness, which is the growing sum of all our new tools and understanding, must be constantly maintained like any good, useful structure. For this reason, the faithful observance of a daily routine is absolutely paramount.

In regards to these goals, there are certain very helpful adjustments we can make. You'd like to get into a great law school? That's wonderful. Rather than envision your goal as, I want to get into Columbia School of Law, frame the goal as I want to do everything I can to make myself the best candidate possible to get into Columbia School of Law. See the difference? You're not even hedging against disappointment. You're actually stating the goal as clearly as possible, emphasizing the aspects you have control over, your qualifications and your application. Your goal is not being accepted; that's out of your control. What's within your control is making your best case, that's your goal.

This extends to so many of a Stoic's secondary goals. My goal is to present my best case to...the potential investor...that guy I like, etc. Or, if you're an athlete, say, my goal is to run my best race or play my best game, rather than simply demolish the competition.

Separate your goals into those things you have the most control over. Remove from yourself the illusion that you have some control over the results. You don't. It's not an excuse for not setting goals. It's a clarifying practice that will probably help advance your goal. But, then again, maybe not.

Imagine Absence, Imagine What You Fear

Negative visualization is a powerful tool of meditation that can help you better reach into many Stoic principles. Some Stoics have claimed it's even the most powerful freeing tool they use on a daily basis. To fully appreciate, they say, all the things you have which you value, imagine yourself without them. Conversely, all those things you fear, imagine them happening. I believe Hollywood understands both sides of this equation. For that matter, so did the ancient Greeks, but maybe they took it one step further. For their annual festivals celebrating Dionysus, the daily theatrical program always included horribly bloody tragedies alternating with light-hearted and goofy satyr plays where the girl got the boy or some combination thereof, and everybody lived happily ever after, or at least sometimes.

Say you live in California, and your house straddles the famous San Andreas fault. Most people would say it's time to move, but you can't afford to. So you're stuck living in dread of the big one. And it's coming, that's for sure. But hopefully, after you've finally been able to move back to Kansas where earthquakes are infrequent. (We could talk about tornadoes then.) But here you're living in dread of the big quake coming and that house, with you in it, falling down into a fissure of molten lava.

Even if the fear was an unreasonable one, this meditative practice says just imagine that fear as completely as you can. Likewise, all the other fears you may have, imagine yourself suffering the worst of them. Take all those nagging, pestering little fears too. Put them all into the forefront of consciousness and let your imagination give them a full shape, let them play out as best as you can picture it.

Surely some such principle is at work when we see a horror movie, a disaster movie, or even an ancient Athenian tragedy, where you just know that very thing our hero is doing everything in his or her power to avoid just seems to lead directly into the very thing itself.

It's a kind of purifying. Fear, when let out to play a little, behaves better afterward.

Extend this to a simple absence. What would your life be without that amazing partner, great kids, and friends? Don't worry about Tesla; it's not that important. But imagine yourself without all those others who give meaning and depth to your life. You're the last person on earth, not even a single zombie trying to get at you. Just entirely alone.

But you're not. It's just a thought experiment. Maybe it will take you to a state of gratitude for what you're truly fortunate to have. Sort of like that happy ending Hollywood knows is worth an extra twenty percent at the box office.

The Stoics got, and still get, a pretty bad rap as being pessimistic, but there's nothing further from the truth. Stoics are actually the world's most persistent optimists. Stoics just go well beyond looking at the proverbial glass half full or glass half empty argument. We examine the nature of the cup itself and end up grateful that such a miraculous and useful object exists.

And don't we experience grief and loss at many points in our life anyway? How sad it truly is when it's only at that point of actual loss that we realize the full value and meaning of the loss. Isn't it preferable to be able to say, when a loss occurs, that we had fully enjoyed and appreciated that which was taken?

Everything Is not as It Should Be: Count Your Blessings

"Everything we have is borrowed."

- Seneca

All those things and people we have in our life, even that Tesla, even that perfect spouse, and that place where we buy ice cream as well as the ice cream itself, are on loan to us and could be taken at any time. As we've conceded and continue to concede often, even our very selves, minds included, are ephemeral and will someday be gone. This also includes all those things we hold most dear, and which give us the deepest joy and satisfaction. And that doesn't include the car.

It's certainly easier to see this with regards to our material possessions, our wealth, even our so-called reputations, which we often invest so much energy in, how we believe others should see us; but everything will eventually be gone from us. Philosophically, this is perhaps the most difficult truth of all to accept. What remains behind us long after those who might remember us are gone too, and those who remember them are gone as well? Very little, it seems.

But do we then throw up our hands in defeat and say, I give up, nothing matters, there's no basis for life? Do we bury our heads in the sand? Do we return to the life of endless distraction and mindless consumption, even though that never really worked for us?

The Stoic accepts reality as it is. This is the primary virtue, honesty, and truth. But isn't the sweetness we know when we live a useful life a kind of truth? Isn't it a truth we can apprehend in our mind, set as a primary goal and work towards, and then construct a satisfying life around?

Not everybody has what it takes to be a true Stoic, to be that person who can walk to the very edge of the cliff, stand there undisturbed by fear, and see the view for what it is. I'd suggest that probably few do. But as we deepen our Stoic practice, as one comes to the deepest states of acceptance while looking out at that view at cliff's edge, we see interior and exterior vistas as stunning and awe-inspiring as exist anywhere in human experience. Rather than be filled with gloom and pessimism, we're filled with purpose and optimism. The true wonder of ourselves and those around us come into focus. We become deeply grateful for our blessings in our brief time here, and so we count them often. Gratitude and humility become almost one and the same.

Take a daily account of those things you have, yourself, and those around you, knowing how brief the time is you have with them. Say your goodbyes as if it could be the last time you'll ever see them, your hellos as if some great gift has been bestowed, regard your time in their presence as if a long-sought prize has been won for it truly has. This is the gift the practice of Stoic principles will lead you to apprehend with clarity. You're part of the ever-flowing wonder of life. Everything is not as it should be, but as it is.

Chapter 9: Further Reading and Stoic Sayings

Some Further Reading

As we've noted earlier, the most widely distributed of the ancient Stoic philosophy is Marcus Aurelius, former Emperor of Rome, god bless his little heart. There are several very good translations of his Meditations usually available at any of the large chain bookstores. Having a heavily thumbed-through copy of this book always on your bed stand is required for any self-respecting Stoic.

The Enchiridion (Notebook) of Epictetus is the other strongly suggested text. It's a short manual that was compiled by his favorite student, Arrian, the one who took excellent notes. And it's much more succinct than Meditations, which is denser (some claim a little rambling), due it seems to its creation as a personal meditative guide. But The Enchiridion is a concise compendium of practical Stoic precepts, bits of which I've included at the end of this chapter.

There are several extant works from the ancient Roman philosopher, Stoic, and playwright, Seneca, which I would suggest when you want to take an even deeper plunge.

Among twentieth century Stoics, I would recommend Viktor Frankl's Man's Search For Meaning. While it's not necessarily a treatise on Stoicism, and Frankl is also a man many have been critical of, it's surely the most extreme example of how Stoic principles endured under the most harrowing conditions.

How To Be A Stoic, by Massimo Pigliucci is perhaps the best work on modern Stoicism by a modern practitioner and the most up to date. It was only recently published.

There is also an ever-increasing flow of publications, blogs, and dedicated social media accounts on the topic. There's no shortage of lively and informed discussion. I strongly suggest anyone starting a Stoic practice to jump in and get involved, find new Stoic friends. You might try to influence them, but don't try to control them.

Some Quotes from Epictetus

"Do well what you're able to do, take everything else as it comes."

"The man who is content with what he has is wise, foolish if he grieves for what he does not have."

"The reason we have two ears and only one mouth is so we can listen twice as much as we speak."

"First know yourself, and only then dress yourself."

"Understand first what you mean to say, then say it."

"Tolerate all religions…every man must find heaven their own way."

"Freedom isn't purchasing everything you want, but controlling the desire to purchase."

"The intention of Nature is this: to bring together in harmony the right action with the useful."

Some Quotes from Marcus Aurelius

"Speak plainly to all and say the same both to the many as you say to one man and without regard to their rank or status. The truth doesn't change according to the listener."

"A man always wishes to get away from wherever he is: to the country house; the seashore; the mountains. But this is the desire of the foolish and thoughtless man. There already exists within himself a perfect place of retreat and repose. For nowhere else it is there more peace and calm than there is within himself. This is especially so for that man who lives truly. He already has a place of perfect rest, a mind that is well-ordered and free from conflict and disturbance."

"Reflect often on how the mind exists apart from even your breathing, whether you breathe hard or soft. Your mind has the power to leave your body and find its own expression."

Some Quotes From Seneca

"All cruelty comes from weakness."

"Consider that each and every day is like a single life unto itself."

"True satisfaction comes from the present moment. The future has yet to occur. Don't distract yourself with fear of the future, but live in the present and you will lack nothing."

"Yet always we complain that life is brief, though we act as if our days would have no end."

"When young strive to remember well those things which inspired you. When you are old, you'll be better able to know them."

"If a man doesn't know where he is going, he'll never arrive there."

"The lust for money enslaves both the wealthy and the poor."

"A life can't be considered a failure if it's been lived with honor. No matter how brief or long, an honorable life is complete."

"Perhaps the desire for fame and applause will bother you. But often think about how everything is soon forgotten. Think how infinite the sweep of time is and how empty this applause is. Think also of how often the nature of those who give applause changes. Who are these whose praise you seek?"

"How much trouble you avoid when looking to see what others say or think, but just which you yourself do or think."

"Should you be standing beside a clear, running stream and curse it, rather than drink from it, does the stream stop flowing? If you throw dirt into it, does it not quickly get carried off? How then can you possess such a stream within yourself? You do by living hourly in the freedom of living modestly, with contentment and simplicity."

"Even though we are social creatures, each man is yet the only master of one, himself. If it weren't so, wouldn't another's wickedness by my wickedness? For this reason, nature has ordered it so. My happiness depends upon no other man."

"Think often about this: What is the nature of the entire whole of the world? And what is your own nature that lives within that wholeness of the world? And yet, is there anything that stops you from acting in that world according to your best understanding of yourself?"

" A certain limit of time is fixed for your life. Use it to clear away the confusion of your mind. The limit will soon be reached. There will not be another chance."

"How is it that every man loves himself most of all, but then values the opinions of others over his own opinion of himself?"

www.ingramcontent.com/pod-product-compliance
Lightning Source LLC
Chambersburg PA
CBHW070645220526
45466CB00001B/304